Understanding Autism in Adults and Aging Adults

Improving Diagnosis and Quality of Life

Theresa M. Regan, Ph.D., CAS

Neuropsychologist
Certified Autism Specialist

Understanding Autism in Adults and Aging Adults Copyright
2016 © Theresa Regan PhD

Paperback ISBN - 9781946824004
Hardback ISBN - 9781946824011
Ebook ISBN - 9781946824028

Published in the United States of America
INDIEGO PUBLISHING LLC
Think Indie. Go Create. Publish.

Editing and Interior Design: Janet Angelo
www.indiegopublishing.com

Cover Design: Rachel Lopez, www.r2cdesign.com

Also written by Theresa Regan:
Soul Cries
2013 National Indie Excellence Award Finalist
www.adultandgeriatricautism.com

Publisher's Cataloging-In-Publication Data:
Names: Regan, Theresa M.
Title: Understanding autism in adults and aging adults : improving
diagnosis and quality of life / Theresa M. Regan, Ph.D., CAS,
Neuropsychologist, Certified Autism Specialist.
Description: IndieGo Publishing LLC, [2017] | Includes
bibliographical references.
Identifiers: ISBN 978-1-946824-00-4 (paperback) | ISBN
978-1-946824-01-1 (hardback) | ISBN 978-1-946824-02-8 (ebook)
Subjects: LCSH: Autistic people. | Autism--Diagnosis. | Autism in
adulthood.
Classification: LCC RC553.A88 R44 2017 (print) | LCC RC553.A88
(ebook) | DDC 616.85882--dc23

Dedication and Acknowledgments

I dedicate this book to my tribe:

The musicians who sing life into my projects,
The listeners who tell me what you hear,
The tenders of the fire who keep the flame burning.

I would like to acknowledge all of the individuals and
families navigating the sometimes beautiful and
sometimes treacherous road of autism across the
lifespan.
You are the inspiration for this book.

I thank and recognize Janet Angelo for editing and
publishing the book. Her thread helps tie it all together.

My deepest thanks and gratitude to my family for your
support.

And to my husband Patrick and my son Joshua, you
bless me always.

Table of Contents

When Medication Can Help

Chapter 1

Adult Autism Spectrum Disorder: Not Just a Label

Dr. Frank referred seventy-two-year-old Mrs. Canady to my clinic for a dementia assessment. Her husband and children accompanied her to discuss behaviors of concern. They noted that she had unusual beliefs that persisted even when they attempted to dissuade her through solid reasoning and evidence. She had no mental health history, and her check-up of thinking skills in our office was completely normal.

During further in-depth conversations with Mrs. Canady and her family, it became clear that she had always had a reputation for being a good listener. She listened intently when others were speaking, but she rarely contributed.

All throughout her life, she had demonstrated unusual beliefs and had struggled to understand the motives of others. Mrs. Canady thought that certain events were deeply meaningful, events that others considered mundane, everyday occurrences.

Her family noted that she had trouble being organized at home, but she was also quite particular and compulsive with certain aspects of housekeeping.

Mrs. Canady appeared pleasant at the appointment and answered my questions freely and openly. She denied having concerns, fears, or sadness. She was taking antipsychotics and antidepressants, and had undergone electroconvulsive treatments for presumed new onset depression with psychotic features, all without any improvement in symptoms.

Given these factors and many other details provided by the patient's family, I began to wonder about the presence of certain autism spectrum symptoms, which perhaps had become more prominent with age. Although I did not feel certain she met the full criteria for Autism Spectrum Disorder (ASD), I called the referring physician to discuss this diagnostic possibility and the impact it might have on her treatment.

Dr. Frank let me know that he did not believe Mrs. Canady could be in the spectrum because she was married. (Although there is truth in the belief that individuals in the autism spectrum have fewer intimate relationships than neurotypical individuals, Dr. Frank believed the myth that this one feature alone can determine a diagnosis). He added, "I'm not really interested in autism spectrum because I'm not a pediatric physician. I just want to make sure she doesn't have dementia."

My name is Dr. Theresa Regan, and I am a neuropsychologist. I specialize in understanding how the brain's physical structure and function are linked to thinking skills, emotions, personality, and behavior. I have worked in hospitals for over twenty-five years and performed check-ups of brain function in patients with a variety of conditions including dementia, brain injury, infectious diseases, medical confusion, and more. I serve patients ranging in age from the teen years through more advanced ages.

I am a mother. My son was diagnosed in the autism spectrum when he was five years old. He does not have intellectual impairment, and is in a regular classroom at school. As a family, we have participated in many assessments and interventions related to autism. On a day-to-day basis, I have had the privilege of living with my son, seeing his gifts and strengths, and observing the symptoms and challenges as well. Autism is real to me in a way that it may not be to clinicians who have not experienced it in a loved one.

I am a Certified Autism Specialist. Although I had many years of experience in the area of brain-behavior relationships before my son was born, my world opened to new knowledge and understanding of these functions when my husband and I experienced what the developmental condition of autism is like in a child. My experience as a neuropsychologist and a mother have merged and motivated me to pursue training and practical experience in the area of autism with the completion of this additional certification. I am now attuned to the symptoms of autism across the lifespan, and I am aware of the barriers to identifying autism at all stages of life.

Dr. Frank in the scenario above verbalized what many of us think when we hear that someone we know might have autism. Our first reaction is to assume that surely something else must be wrong, something that can be easily managed with a medication or counseling perhaps. We tell ourselves that ASD can be ruled out because the patient readily makes eye contact or enjoys close relationships such as a thriving, happy marriage. But it goes well beyond this. Medical professionals need to know how to recognize autism spectrum disorder in children and in adults of all ages, as ASD is a lifelong condition. It does not disappear with age, and thus, correct diagnosis is absolutely key to improving quality of life.

As with Dr. Frank, however, many doctors assume that if a patient has autism, surely it would have been identified by the school system or a pediatrician when the patient was a child. In that case, it would already be in the patient's medical record. It can't apply to my daughter, spouse, or patient, because my daughter makes eye contact, my spouse has a job, and my patient is a grandmother. Even if autism does apply, what difference would it make? Shouldn't we leave well enough alone? Autism can't be cured, and giving someone such a "radical" new diagnosis might stigmatize him/her.

What is Autism Spectrum Disorder (ASD)?

Although autism has become a well-known term, it is a relatively new diagnosis. In the 1940s, Dr. Leo Kanner from Johns Hopkins University described withdrawn behavior in children as "autistic." Around the same time, Dr. Hans Asperger, a German scientist and pediatrician, described a similar constellation of symptoms in children.

In the first Diagnostic and Statistical Manual published in 1952 (the diagnostic classification system published by the American Psychiatric Association), children could be identified as having schizophrenic reaction/childhood type with characteristic withdrawn behavior.

In the second edition of the DSM published in 1968, the diagnosis of schizophrenia/childhood type included "autistic, atypical, and withdrawn behavior; failure to develop identity separate from mother's; and general unevenness, gross immaturity, and inadequacy in development. These developmental defects may result in mental retardation, which should also be diagnosed."

Autism as a distinct category of diagnosis was not included in the DSM until the third edition published in 1980, and was labeled "infantile autism." Criteria included decreased social responsiveness with onset prior to thirty months of age, language impairment (absent language or peculiar speech patterns), unusual behavioral reactions (resistance to change, peculiar interests, or attachment to objects), and the absence of delusions or hallucinations characteristic of schizophrenia.

A revised edition of DSM-III was published in 1987 with more observable and specific developmental behaviors within three categories of impaired social interaction, communication, and imaginative activity, and markedly restricted activities and interests.

In 1994, the DSM-IV introduced several terms to describe individuals under the autism umbrella, including Rett's Disorder, Childhood Disintegrative Disorder, Pervasive Developmental Disorder (NOS), Asperger's Disorder, and Autistic Disorder.

In the most recent version of the DSM (fifth edition, 2013), Autism Spectrum Disorder (ASD) is the only term used. Below, I have paraphrased the criteria in list form. (Please refer to the formal criteria in the DSM-5 for original wording.) Additionally, I have added a patient example (Joseph) to demonstrate how the criteria may look in a real-world example.

The criteria are presented in the DSM-5 with examples for illustration. The examples are not meant to be exhaustive. I have provided these examples as a checklist for ease of use.

Criteria for Diagnosing ASD

Each of the following **three** criteria must be met. These describe persistent difficulties with social communication and interactions across multiple contexts:

1. ### Deficits in social-emotional reciprocity

   ✓ Abnormal social approach
   ✓ Inability to engage in the back-and-forth nature of true conversation
   ✓ Reduced sharing of interests or emotions
   ✓ Failure to initiate or respond to social interactions

Joseph was a fifty-eight-year-old gentleman who presented for assessment of possible autism spectrum disorder. When I met with Joseph, he was very talkative and difficult to keep on topic. Once he was off topic, he was resistant to my attempts to redirect him, and he often started long and complex stories that he strongly wished to finish.

He began speaking about sports statistics, and I said, "My favorite sport is baseball." He said, "Uh-huh. The first thing I ever researched was college football. Did you know that the early football games at Harvard and Princeton were largely unorganized? There were lots of different rules." His sister and brother told me that he often seems to talk just to hear himself talk, "but he doesn't really want you to say anything most of the time."

2. ### Deficits in nonverbal communicative behaviors used for social interaction

   ✓ Poorly connected verbal and nonverbal communication
   ✓ Abnormalities in eye contact or body language
   ✓ Deficits in understanding and using gestures in a meaningful way to improve communication
   ✓ Lack of facial expressions and other forms of nonverbal communication

Joseph made some eye contact during the session, but he also looked at the ceiling when he talked about sports. I suggested that I would like him to say, "You did a good job with that" in a happy and encouraging tone. This was quite easy for him. I then asked him to say those same words using a sarcastic tone. He thought about this for a moment then said it with flat emotion, seeming unsure of how to convey sarcasm.

Joseph's family noted that he often used the same enthusiastic tone of voice for all topics and settings without appropriate range of prosody (emotions and tone of voice). They noted that he seemed to lack an understanding of the emotional tone of others during conversations, such as determining from his sister's tone of voice whether she was angry with him or just curious about something. He often didn't understand jokes that depended on the speaker's inflection of words and the rhythm of delivery. In contrast, Joseph liked to tell jokes because he was in charge of the delivery and knew the humor he was trying to convey. His siblings said that his attempts at being humorous were sometimes quite funny and other times very awkward.

3. Deficits in developing, maintaining, and understanding relationships

- ✓ Difficulty adjusting behavior to various social contexts
- ✓ Difficulty sharing imaginative play or making friends
- ✓ Decreased or absent interest in peers

Joseph had never married and had no children. He had lived in a small apartment in a small town for most of his life. He had worked at a simple job, finding his niche writing sports copy for a television news station. He was well known in the community but was not close to anyone in particular. He visited his sister once a year.

When I asked him who he was closest to, he stated, "You mean who do I live near?" When asked again about who he shared a close relationship with, he stated, "Well, probably my mother, but she is dead now."

Two of the following **four** criteria must be met. These describe narrow and repetitive patterns of behavior or interests. The symptoms may be current or in the patient's history:

1. **Stereotyped or repetitive movements of the body, use of objects, or speech**

   ✓ Motor stereotypies
   ✓ Lining up or flipping objects repetitively
   ✓ Repeating words and phrases
   ✓ Using idiosyncratic language (words with private meaning, made-up words)

Joseph had a history of echolalia as a child. He would say something and then repeat himself, such as "I'm coming, I'm coming," or "Don't put that there! Not there, not there." As an adult, he demonstrated some motor stereotypies such as pacing the length of his apartment and making repetitive, exaggerated mouth movements when stressed.

2. **Insistence on sameness, inflexible adherence to routines, or rituals of behavior**

   ✓ Extreme distress at small changes
   ✓ Difficulty with transitions
   ✓ Rigid thinking patterns
   ✓ Greeting rituals
   ✓ Need to take the same route or eat the same foods every day

Once a year, Joseph visited his sister who lived several hours away. He visited during the same week of July without variation. When he got there, he was very set on visiting the same five places he always visited in her town including a museum and an observatory. One year, the museum was closed for construction, and Joseph was extremely stressed. He paced throughout the house moaning and wringing his hands. It was several hours before he calmed down, and for the remainder of his stay, he talked about not being able to visit the museum. Family members also noticed that he used the greeting "Howdy hoo" regardless of the situation, whether greeting his young niece, the family priest, or a police officer.

3. **Highly restricted, fixated interests that are abnormal in intensity or focus**

   ✓ Strong attachment to or preoccupation with unusual objects
   ✓ Excessively restricted interests
   ✓ Significant repetition of activity within specific interest areas

In addition to his strong interest in sports statistics and trivia, his apartment was filled with stacks of paper. He was able to give away clothes and household items that he no longer used, but was extremely attached to paper items including old receipts, flyers that came in the mail, and old newspapers. There was no identified reason for his attachment to these papers, and the clutter in the apartment posed a danger to his health and his ability to move throughout the apartment without stumbling or falling.

4. **Hyper- or hypo-reactivity to sensory input, or unusual interests in sensory aspects of the environment**

- ✓ Apparent indifference to pain/temperature
- ✓ Becoming upset or overwhelmed by sounds or textures
- ✓ Excessive smelling or touching of objects
- ✓ Visual fascination with lights or movement

Joseph only wore cotton t-shirts (short sleeves) and sweatpants regardless of the weather or where he was going. He complained that sweaters and jeans were "scratchy." He was very overwhelmed by noise and became agitated if his neighbors were "too loud." On the other hand, he seemed oblivious to pain and hygiene issues, and did not notice when he needed to brush his teeth or when he got scrapes or bruises.

Joseph had lived his fifty-eight years without a correct diagnosis of autism. He had gotten by during his school years because his intellect was fairly good, even though he was slow in completing projects, and he generally achieved Cs. He had gotten by during most of his adulthood years because he had found a niche in a small community that seemed to keep an eye out for him. He had never excelled in academics or advanced in his career, but he really hadn't struggled quite so much until recent years.

By the time he came to see me, he was losing his eyesight and no longer able to work. His brother and sister had moved him to a small apartment closer to them and were attempting to figure out what kind of community services he needed. Although the diagnostic features had been present all his life, they were more of a barrier now that he was aging and his health was diminishing. When I met with Joseph and his family, they asked how he could have gone all these years without a correct diagnosis.

Why Some Individuals Lack a Correct Diagnosis

How did Joseph slip through the diagnostic cracks? Well, when we consider the number of years it took to develop the concept of autism spectrum as a diagnosis, it is clear that many adults alive today grew up in a culture that had no diagnosis or a very limited understanding of autism. Joseph, for example, was nearly thirty years old when the diagnosis was first established in the 1980s.

Secondly, Joseph had normal intellectual skills, whereas individuals who did receive a diagnosis in the early years of the formal diagnostic criteria generally had significant intellectual disability in combination with autism. Unfortunately, even in the 1990s, the period during which I was doing my graduate work, we learned that 75 to 80 percent of autistics were "mentally retarded" (now known as intellectual disability). There was no understanding of what autism looks like across all levels of intellectual function. Indeed, according to a 2014 CDC publication, almost half (46 percent) of children identified with ASD were found to have average to above average intellectual ability. Individuals with intact intellectual ability are often missed when diagnosing ASD.

If Joseph had been recognized as having autism in his younger years, it would not have been understood as a neurodevelopmental condition with a basis in the brain. From the 1940s through most of the 1990s, many prominent authors and scientists attributed autism to parenting issues. These included a description of "refrigerator mothers," mothers who did not give appropriate warmth to their children. Some writers even compared life with a "refrigerator mother" to life in a concentration camp, and surmised that this lack of maternal warmth caused autism.

The lack of any diagnostic criteria, the wrongly assumed connection with intellectual disability, and the incorrect theories about the cause of autism as a parenting deficit all contributed to generations of autistic individuals lacking the appropriate interventions and assistance.

Although we usually hear about autism in children, most clinicians believe that ASD in adults today is just as common, but the diagnosis was less likely to have been made during their childhood because of the lack of information available at the time. Indeed, researchers in England (Brugha, et al., 2011) studied 7,461 adult participants, and found that the prevalence of ASD was about 10 per 1000 and did not differ across age groups. Many of the adults identified in the study had not previously been diagnosed in the spectrum. Brugha and colleagues concluded that adults and geriatric individuals are often unidentified and undiagnosed.

Let us not assume, however, that because there is an increasing awareness of autism in our communities, children are immune from missing an appropriate diagnosis. Research with children in school systems has identified many students who are undiagnosed or misdiagnosed.

A 2009 study in England (Baron-Cohen, et al.) screened all school-aged children and completed thorough assessments with those identified as having possible ASD symptoms. The authors concluded that their results "highlight the reality that there are children with autism spectrum conditions, notably children with high-functioning autism, who remain undetected in primary schools." The authors reported that for every three students identified as having ASD, two were unidentified.

Similarly, in 2011, Kim, Young, Shin, et al., studied a general population sample of students aged seven to twelve years in regular schools and classrooms as well as a high probability group of children in special education programs or currently receiving psychiatric services.

The results indicated that two-thirds of the ASD students in the general population sample were undiagnosed and untreated. The prevalence of ASD in the regular classrooms was reported as 1.89

percent, whereas it was 0.75 percent in the high-probability group. The general education group had more ASD females than the high probability group. Furthermore, 12 percent of ASD students in the general population sample had superior IQs, and 16 percent had intellectual disability.

"We examined the striking finding that many of the children in our study were in regular schools without having been diagnosed and without [receiving] support [services]." (Kim, Young, Shin, et al.)

It is now clear that many children and adults lack an appropriate diagnosis. However, it is important to understand that in addition to those who lack a diagnosis, many individuals in the spectrum carry an incorrect diagnosis. In her article "The Missing Generation" (2015), Jessica Wright wrote, "In the 1950s and 1960s, thousands of children who had autism were either completely missed or were saddled with the wrong label."

Wright describes that in 2009, the Pennsylvania Bureau of Autism Services asked David Mandell, Associate Professor of Psychiatry and Pediatrics at the University of Pennsylvania, to study the epidemiology of autism conditions in institutions within the state. In assessing residents at Norristown State Hospital, a psychiatric institution, he developed such stringent criteria that he "almost biased the process to not find autism." His research team found that 10 percent of the residents had undiagnosed autism and a misdiagnosis of a mental health condition, often schizophrenia. He noted that misdiagnosis leads to mistreatment.

"The fact that they were being treated for a disorder they didn't have—and that their treatment wasn't working—was obvious in the files," he wrote . "One of the big stories here is that there are people out there who are misdiagnosed."

Likewise, Joseph Piven, Professor of Psychiatry at the University of North Carolina at Chapel Hill, notes the challenge involved in identifying and correctly supporting ASD individuals in older generations. "This is just a huge area of no knowledge," he states. "There's almost nothing written about autism and geriatric populations."

Another group of ASD individuals who frequently escape accurate detection are females. Dr. Tony Attwood, a psychologist in Queensland, Australia, and the author of numerous books and papers on Asperger's syndrome (a DSM-IV diagnosis often given to ASD individuals with functional intellectual skills), has written about the under-diagnosis of autism in girls without severe intellectual disability. He notes that, although the core characteristics of ASD are the same in women, the way the symptoms present may be different.

In order to create a sense of self, some girls and women read fantasy fiction, create personas, write fiction, or create imaginary friends. There may be a focus on ancient and current civilizations around the world, and thinking about where she believes she might feel at home or fit in. In addition, she may focus on mythology, fairies, or witches as a way to think about a crafting a different life for herself or gaining special powers as a coping mechanism.

Dr. Attwood notes that the adoption of personas as a way of navigating the struggle of social interaction "can lead clinicians to suspect characteristics of Multiple Personality Disorder" or "can lead to suspicions that signs of schizophrenia can be developing."

One of my own patients described it this way: "I feel like a chameleon. I just mimic the personality of the person I'm talking to."

Family and clinicians may wonder if the ASD individual is in touch with reality. As Dr. Attwood explains, "An adolescent or young adult [with ASD] may only come to the attention of clinicians for the diagnostic assessment of a secondary mood or personality disorder or psychosis."

In clinical practice, it has been my experience that some ASD individuals escape diagnosis until they reach a season of life in which the complexity and demand of their circumstances overwhelms their ability to cope, like Joseph in the previous example. Although the core features have always been present in those individuals, a stressful life event such as the onset of a medical condition, marriage, death of a close family member, or retirement overwhelms the individual's ability to think clearly, attend to personal care, and cope with the everyday stresses of life.

In summary, although autism spectrum disorder is a lifelong neurologic condition, many children and adults escape accurate detection and receive no diagnosis or an incorrect diagnosis. This lack of accurate diagnosis leads to a lack of interventions and support, or to the presence of interventions that are ineffective or potentially harmful.

Why a Diagnosis of ASD Is Vital

Now that we realize that many individuals in pediatric, adult, and geriatric groups are missing the correct diagnosis of ASD, let's focus on whether diagnosis is important and why.

A diagnosis is the way we wrap words around symptoms that tend to cluster together in one person. Instead of describing each characteristic of the person, we can use a few words to communicate significant meaning. Humans need to use language to communicate what is real. This helps us solve problems and understand the context of what is happening in and around us.

It is generally a misplaced assumption that people are better served if we do not "label" them with a diagnosis. In my experience, people label each other regardless of whether it is with a diagnosis or not. The question is not whether people will describe the individual using language, but whether the descriptions will be accurate and helpful.

The ASD individual who is not carrying a correct diagnosis may be labeled as unmotivated, stubborn, lazy, cheap, stingy, or picky, depending on their unique set of traits. Others may incorrectly think that the ASD individual behaves in a certain way because he doesn't care about the feelings of others or isn't motivated to change. A correct diagnosis can help to prevent mislabeling and serve as a way of communicating the truth about a neurologic condition that manifests in emotions, behavior, and social communication.

Some avoid the diagnosis for fear of stigma. However, there is only stigma if we allow stigma. We are the ones who determine how we treat issues of individual diversity. Autism is a neurologic developmental condition that should have no more stigma than heart disease or osteoporosis. If we avoid a correct and helpful diagnosis because we fear stigma, we are the ones feeding the stigma. The more concerned we are with positive outcomes, the more committed we can be to finding a correct diagnosis and making progress for each individual in our communities.

A right diagnosis is important for good outcomes. If an individual has diabetes, a correct diagnosis is critical and drives healthy treatment recommendations. Just so, the correct diagnosis of ASD should also drive appropriate and helpful information and intervention strategies.

An incorrect diagnosis—schizophrenia, depression with psychosis, dementia—often generates inappropriate strategies and interventions. For example, antipsychotics may be used to treat what appear to be delusions but are actually fixed beliefs within the context of autism. The result is a lack of progress in treatment. Additionally, the ASD individual with extreme sleep disturbance may be told to wake up earlier in the day so that s/he can go to sleep earlier at night, but that strategy alone is likely to be unsuccessful for someone in the autism spectrum. An individual may be treated for attention deficit disorder with stimulant medication, but this may increase his/her predominant ASD-related anxiety and cause other problems.

In addition to improving interventions, a correct diagnosis also allows clinicians to improve assessment. For example, because I know that certain qualities often cluster together within the autism spectrum, having the correct diagnosis leads me to look for common associated symptoms. For example, because I know that many in the spectrum eat a small variety of foods repetitively, I know that I should ask them what they eat on a daily basis. The issue of nutrition can impact other medical conditions and overall health. Because I understand that many ASD individuals have sensory symptoms that contribute to anxiety and lack of resilience throughout the day, I know to add sensory interventions to the treatment plan. Knowing one diagnosis leads me to investigate many other common symptoms that can impact health and well-being.

Also, the diagnosis can be very important to the ASD individual's sense of self, community, and belonging. Many individuals in the autism spectrum who have functional intelligence understand that they feel different, and they want to know why. When given a diagnosis, they often describe a great sense of relief because they finally understand the uniqueness of who they are. Following a diagnosis, many experience the joy of making connections with others in the ASD community, and finally being able to relate to others who can understand their life experiences.

This greater understanding also brings context to situations in everyday life. That is, without an understanding of the neurology behind an autistic individual's behavior, many people resort to blame and shame if the behavior seems uncaring or is frustrating to deal with. "Why don't you remember my birthday?" or "I worked hard to cook this meal for dinner. Why won't you even try it?" can be comments that the individual in the autism spectrum hears from others. Without context, the person making these statements incorrectly feels that the ASD individual could easily have behaved differently if only s/he cared enough. The ASD individual may wonder why s/he doesn't behave differently and why s/he can't meet the expectations of others. Both people involved in the interaction feel misunderstood and discouraged.

With a correct diagnosis of autism, there can be a greater understanding that the behaviors of the ASD individual do not have a root in rejection or a lack of caring. Caring is likely to "look different" when expressed by the individual with autism. Also, the autistic individual's needs are often very different from those of the neurotypical person.

Overall, a correct diagnosis leads to better understanding, communication, assessment, and intervention, all of which lead to more successful outcomes.

Why We Need Greater Awareness of ASD Across the Lifespan

Historically, awareness of intellectual disability (ID), formerly known as mental retardation, emerged in the 1800s. There was the dawning knowledge that some individuals had less clear thinking than others. Discussions and programs were developed to determine what could be done for individuals with ID. Currently, many specific criteria of measurement help teachers and agencies understand the types of support an individual with intellectual disability might need to remain as independent as possible while staying safe and healthy.

In contrast, there remains a lack of understanding about the impact of autism on daily functioning. Rather than being a condition involving *intellect*, autism is a neurologic condition involving *behavior*. Although our understanding that the brain impacts thinking skills has evolved, there remains a significant lack of understanding about the connection between the brain and behavior. We remain much more likely to attribute behavioral symptoms to issues of motivation, poor character, or flawed parenting.

Although these issues can impact behavior, there are multiple neurologic conditions that also impact how someone regulates emotion and behavior. In the same way that an understanding of intellectual disability as a brain-based condition created appropriate community supports, we must create a better understanding of what neurologically-based behavioral difficulties—such as those in autism—look like and how they impact daily life. This improved understanding will help to develop appropriate supports and interventions for ASD individuals of all ages.

In the study referenced above, Brugha and colleagues found that adults in the autism spectrum were more likely to be socially disadvantaged, to have lower educational attainment, and to lack access to the community services available to them. They noted that adults with mental health disorders such as depression, schizophrenia, or bipolar disorder tend to receive more community services "because these problems are recognized needs." Brugha et al. added that based on their experience, "social care to adults with a diagnosis of ASD leads to improvements in quality of life and reductions in the inappropriate use of high-cost hospital services."

In addition to the need for awareness of autism in the absence of intellectual disability, there is an increasing need for individuals who understand adult medical and mental health conditions to also be expert in autism. Because of its developmental nature, much of the initial focus on autism has been within the areas of pediatric medicine, early intervention services, and the school systems. Clinicians who specialize in autism, therefore, are almost primarily pediatric specialists. Because autism is a condition across the entire lifespan, clinicians who are expert in adult and geriatric care need to be just as expert as pediatric clinicians in the area of autism diagnosis and services.

The urgency of this need cannot be overstated. There are many undiagnosed adults in our communities, and many children who have been diagnosed with autism who will soon be adults. According to the 2009 publication "The Current State of Services for Adults with Autism," the adults we currently see in our communities represent "only the proverbial tip of the iceberg. Some reports note that 70 percent of the identified individuals with ASD are younger than fourteen years of age. This is a looming crisis of unprecedented magnitude for adults with ASD, their families, and the ill-prepared and underfunded adults' service system charged with meeting their needs."

This book is written for ASD adults who are undiagnosed or newly diagnosed. It is written for the families and clinicians serving these individuals throughout their lifespan. It is written for community workers and policy makers who are looking for a clearer view of the aging autistic individual.

The book is divided into three parts, with the first focusing on an explanation and illustration of core features and associated symptoms of autism along with suggested intervention options.

The second part of the book focuses on issues that are broader in scope than the core features of ASD, issues such as relationships, independent living, employment, and retirement.

The third portion brings together the multiple interventions highlighted in the book and adds two extended case studies as real-life examples.

The time is now. Join me in navigating life through the eyes, heart, and mind of the aging autistic adult.

Chapter 2

Diagnostic and Associated Features of ASD

Eric was a preschooler in a local school that I visited frequently. I saw him on various occasions and knew that the school staff had met repeatedly with Eric's parents about his disruptive behavior. His school team and parents had developed a complex discipline plan to help Eric control his outbursts, all without success. I observed that if someone accidentally touched Eric while he was waiting in line for the water fountain, he lost control and acted out. When walking down the hallway in a line of students, he spun in circles the entire time. One morning, as I walked down the corridor, I heard him crying out, and when I glanced in the window of the classroom door, I saw him rolling on the floor. Other than Eric and the teacher, the classroom was empty. The teacher opened the door and explained that she had moved the students to a separate room for their safety. "I don't know what's wrong with him," she said, the frustration evident in her voice. "Why does he act like this? He's not stupid."

No, Eric was not stupid. He was bright and creative and a wonderful artist. He was also an undiagnosed autistic. When I spoke with his father about my own son and how much developmental therapies had helped him, he said, "Eric's pediatrician says he is fine. She says he will grow out of it." I could sense that the father was not willing to consider that his son might be autistic, and that was the end of the discussion.

I saw Eric three years later at a children's event. The coaches were trying to teach him a sporting technique, and he was not following instructions. In fact, his behavior was very rigid, and he insisted on holding the sporting equipment in his left hand even though he was right handed. The coaches tried to reason with him and discipline him, all without success. I could see that people were baffled by Eric's behavior, especially those who were familiar with his sharp mind and artistic abilities.

Intelligence and Academic Ability

What is intelligence, and how crucial is it to optimal daily functioning? There are a variety of formal definitions of intelligence and even more notions and ideas we hold individually. One might say that intelligence is the ability to acquire and apply knowledge. Others might say it represents an individual's ability to learn and reason.

As a neuropsychologist, I think of intelligence as having quite a bit to do with problem solving and reasoning. Intelligence tends to correlate with standardized exams, academic grades, and the number of academic years completed in one's education. Additionally, higher intelligence increases the probability of success at a job, particularly one that is complex.

Linda Gottfredson states that "no other single predictor measured to date (specific aptitude, personality, education, experience) seems to have such consistently high predictive validities for job performance" as intelligence.

Although having a higher IQ increases the probability of success in certain areas of life, other brain skills also affect success in daily activities. Academic abilities, for example, are separate from intellect. When one's achievement in an area of academics is lower than one's intellect, a learning disability is diagnosed. A reading disability is called dyslexia, and a math disability is called acalculia.

It is common for individuals in the autism spectrum with average or above average intelligence to have uneven abilities across intellect and academics. Verbal problem solving may be quite a bit higher or lower than spatial skills (nonverbal abilities such as assembling a puzzle).

Likewise, there may be a large gap between academic abilities such as reading or math. An individual in the autism spectrum may read very early and at an advanced level, but at the same time may not be able to understand basic math. Others may be a whiz at math, but may graduate high school with the reading ability of a third-grader. The individual may be a gifted artist or pianist but struggle significantly in other areas.

Although some in the spectrum have abilities referred to as savant—a level of ability so strong that it far exceeds other abilities—most autistics have noticeable strengths and weaknesses in intellectual or academic skills. Other areas of brain function are separate from intelligence or academics, but they significantly impact daily functioning.

Memory

Memory is an area of cognitive ability that is separate from intellectual function. Within the autism spectrum, there may be difficulty memorizing certain kinds of information or information that is presented in a certain way. For example, it is common for individuals in the spectrum to have an exceptional memory for details or information obtained through rote memorization, such as phone numbers, dates, names of presidents, and state capitals, whereas neurotypical individuals might have to work quite hard to memorize these.

At the same time, however, the ASD individual often has much more difficulty recalling things that seem to have deeper meaning and importance. For example, many young adults I assess live with their parents but cannot recall what their parents do at work. One young man told me that he has no siblings but has "many family members." When I asked if he could tell me more about his family, he said he knew he had family "somewhere," and he remembered seeing them several times a year, but he couldn't recall if they were cousins, aunts, uncles, or other relatives.

Similarly, the ASD individual may experience increased difficulty in school once she is required to read texts and take notes on lectures. In younger grades, the teacher is more likely to outline specifically what should be memorized for a test. In higher grades, the student is expected to listen to teacher or professor, read a wealth of information on a topic, and identify the key points and concepts. The autistic individual may be able to memorize information but have difficulty knowing what is meaningful or important. For example, an ASD student may be unable to tell that the heading "Three Types of Blood Vessels: Veins, Arteries, and Capillaries" contains information that is more likely to be on the test than the sentence "There are many different shapes and sizes of blood vessels in the body."

Additionally, when the student is given examples of a new concept in class, she may struggle to apply those examples to the examples on the exam if they are even slightly different. Because of the concrete thought process of the ASD student, she may have difficulty knowing that a new example is getting at the same concept she memorized earlier with a different example. She may have a tendency to remember details but be unable to learn concepts and then apply those concepts to other situations and settings (transference of learning).

In addition to having difficulty understanding the meaning and importance of new data, individuals with ASD are likely to have difficulty learning in certain types of environments or conditions. An individual's ability to memorize and learn new information may be good, but the educational setting may be quite distracting or upsetting to the learner. ASD learners are more likely to be distracted by external and internal sensory information than general learners are. For example, the itchy tag in the shirt collar, the noise of the air conditioning system, and the flickering lights in the classroom may make learning difficult.

The speed and format of the information being presented may also be problematic. Some learners with autism feel "pushed" by the speed of information presented, and easily fall behind the lecture topic. ASD students are more likely to be stressed and upset in the midst of their own rigid thought processes. For example, if a student feels that the color blue is very important and meaningful, he may be very distracted that he was given a black notebook instead of the blue one he had last semester. If the teacher usually starts class by reviewing yesterday's homework, but today begins class by talking about a new concept, the ASD learner may feel stressed at this unexpected change.

Other learners in the spectrum have core memory deficits, even in a one-on-one environment, such as with a learning specialist. For example, an individual with autism spectrum disorder may show difficulty taking in and remembering social information, such as remembering a story about something that happened to someone. She may have trouble taking in large chunks of information at once due to a slower thought process. Some ASD learners benefit from the repetition of information. Others benefit from having information presented in a certain way. One individual may do best with pictures and diagrams, while another may be a very verbal and language-based learner. Some do best listening to information while others do best reading the information.

As you can see, memory and learning abilities are important for successful daily functioning. These areas can have specific profiles, particularly in the case of those with developmental disabilities such as ASD. If we only consider intellectual ability or academics, we will overlook ways to help the individual succeed in school, work, and daily life.

Praxis

Praxis is the brain's ability to direct meaningful movements. Even if an individual has the ability to perform a particular movement, he may have significant difficulty bringing several movements together to do something meaningful in daily life. Someone with impaired praxis is said to have dyspraxia or apraxia depending on the severity of difficulty. An individual with dyspraxia may be able to move his arm but not coordinate his arm movements to throw a ball. In other words, he has difficulty "putting the pieces together" to produce a fluid movement to achieve a specific result. If he can throw the ball, it may require conscious thought rather than being an automatic movement.

Dyspraxia is not a diagnostic feature of autism, but, like other developmental symptoms, it occurs at a higher rate in the spectrum than in neurotypical individuals. It can interfere with many everyday activities that most of us take for granted. It can mean an individual isn't able to tie his shoes, swim, or ride a bike. It can mean that when he attempts to throw a ball at a target, the ball goes directly into the ground. Dyspraxia can also impact handwriting to the point of illegibility. It can interfere with someone's ability to draw or put together a bike for his child's Christmas present.

Sometimes delayed speech in children is due to dyspraxia of speech rather than a core language problem. When this is the case, the child often starts speaking very fluently once the dyspraxia improves, whereas the individual with core language problems moves ahead slowly in terms of speaking, using correct grammar in written and spoken language, and sentence construction.

Dyspraxia can also impact dressing skills such as pulling a shirt over her head, managing buttons and zippers, or wrapping a towel around her body after a shower. Dancing and walking downstairs with alternating feet also require some praxis ability. Therefore, praxis is another puzzling part of brain function that can lead others to believe that the ASD individual isn't "trying hard enough" to do a certain skill, is "stupid," or is "goofing off."

It is important to understand that the person who can name the presidents in order may not be able to tie her shoes.

Sleep

Sleep disturbance is a common associated feature in the autism spectrum. Williams et al. describe prevalence estimates of 44 to 83 percent for sleep disorders in this population. They reported the most common sleep difficulties as sleep onset (the ability to fall asleep), restless sleep, and frequent waking. The only significant difference between ASD children with intellectual disability and those with average to high intellectual ability was more frequent nighttime waking in children with lower intellectual abilities.

In my clinical experience, ASD individuals who have sleep disturbance tend to be night owls with a tendency toward a skewed sleep cycle. They often report going to bed around two or three in the morning and sleeping until around noon. It does not matter if they attempt to change their natural cycle by forcing wakefulness in the morning. They still cannot induce sleep at an earlier time at night. Sleep disturbance is one of the areas within the spectrum for which medications and/or supplements are helpful.

Working in conjunction with a physician to find a nighttime medication to help with sleep onset can be very important, as the individual who cannot change his sleep cycle to normative patterns can have difficulty being on time for doctors' appointments, connecting with others in the community, and attending school or work. Lack of sleep can also further decrease the emotional and behavioral resilience of the ASD individual during the day, leading to decreased attention and increased anxiety, shutting down, or emotional outbursts.

Motor Stereotypies

Motor stereotypies are defined in the DSM as "apparently purposeless, rhythmical, repetitive movements." Stereotypies can fulfill a portion of the diagnostic criteria labeled as "stereotyped or repetitive motor movements." Although stereotypies generally have a volitional component, meaning the person can start or stop the movement when asked, these movements are very difficult to suppress over a long period. Like other movement disorders, their expression can be impacted by emotional and physical states such as fatigue, excitement, stress, or anxiety.

These stereotypies are more common in individuals with autism than in those with other developmental conditions. Although some of the examples of stereotypies are common in the general population, they tend to be more intrusive and compulsive within the autism spectrum.

Examples of stereotypies can be found across body parts:

- **Face**: may include opening and closing eyes in an exaggerated movement pattern, gazing out of a corner of the eye at objects or fingers, opening mouth, chewing, grimacing with bared teeth, teeth grinding, sniffing, or sequences of lip and tongue movements.

- **Head and trunk**: repetitive head movements such as tilting, shaking, or nodding; arching or bending the back; shoulder shrugging and trunk rocking, either side to side or forward and back

- **Arms and legs**: flapping movements; crossing, stamping, or pounding the arms or legs

- **Fingers**: finger drumming, tapping, or counting the fingers in sequence; waving or clapping; nail biting; hair twisting; twirling or writhing the hands and wrists; opening and closing the hands

- **Gait** (walking patterns): pacing, skipping, spinning, running, jumping

- **Use of objects**: tapping, shaking, or twirling an object; clicking a pen, snapping a bracelet, twisting a necklace

- **Behaviors**: mouthing words, typing conversations with fingers without the presence of a keyboard, eye or mouth rubbing, covering the ears or smelling objects, banging of the head or extremities, chin tapping, masturbating or touching the genitals in public

In addition to motor stereotypies, a portion of the criteria can be met in the presence of other repetitive behaviors such as lining up toys or flipping objects, echolalia, and using idiosyncratic language.

Echolalia

Echolalia is the repetition of spoken words without reason, purpose, or context to the communication. The repetition may be of something said by another person, or a repetition of an individual's own words. Sometimes the echolalia is overt: "I need to go to town. I need to go to town."

At other times, a person may change the phrase to make it seem that the repetition was meant to emphasize what was said: "I need to go to town. Gotta go to town for a while." This masking can occur when the individual has some insight that he or she has the compulsion to repeat words or phrases, but knows that doing so is not socially acceptable or might cause him/her to seem odd. S/he does this to create a context or to explain the context of the repeated phrase. One individual in the spectrum explained, "I have a craving to say things again."

Idiosyncratic Phrases

Some individuals with autism invent words, such as calling the painted lines on the road pollywoggles, or they change the meanings of commonly used words and have a rigid insistence on using them their way. For example, a person may understand the difference between the words up and down but rigidly insist that everyone around them use down for up and up for down.

Idiosyncratic language can also be unusual ways of using words to describe things. For example, an individual may bump her knee on a piece of furniture and say, "That brown table made my skeleton hurt." It is not hard for someone else to intuit what is being communicated, but that isn't how most people would describe bumping a knee. Another idiosyncrasy can occur with pronouns and possessives, called relational speech. For example, the individual may say, "Can you help my cup?" when she means, "My hands are full, and I'm about to drop my cup. Can you help me open the door?" or "Help the computer" instead of "I need help using the computer."

Repetitive Greetings and Transitional Routines

Certain individuals may appear to do well when greeting others or changing tasks. However, with ongoing observation, it becomes clear that the behaviors are rigid and repetitive rather than spontaneous reactions to the situation. For example, the individual may always say, "Catch ya later" when ending a conversation or "Hello, how are you today?" when greeting someone. These phrases aren't bad, and in many situations work well. However, "Catch ya later" may not be a great way of ending an interview for a legal secretary position, and "Hello, how are you today?" may not be a great way of greeting someone you are visiting in the hospital who just survived a car accident, but his wife did not.

Additionally, the repetition can also involve behavior rather than speech. When leaving the house, an ASD individual may insist on petting the dog, checking the mailbox, and checking all four tires before leaving. Although these are appropriate behaviors when spontaneous, a rigid adherence to this specific routine is problematic on many occasions and time consuming on every occasion.

The ASD individual may demonstrate rigidity in the order in which they perform routine tasks. An insistence that a certain behavior or task be completed in a specific way on every occasion is common among those in the autism spectrum. For example, the person may be independent with her morning routine, but fall apart if she can't brush her teeth before she takes a shower rather than after. Another individual may become extremely stressed if he is diverted through a detour on his way to work.

Intense preoccupation with certain thoughts or topics is also common. This characteristic may involve an intense focus on the symmetry of objects or lining up objects in relation to a shelf edge or in relation to objects next to them. For example, the individual may insist that all objects on the table touch an edge. This intense preoccupation may also manifest in repetitive actions such as drawing, building, or writing. The individual may demonstrate extreme attachment to certain activities and interests, such as watching the weather channel, reading books about Egypt, and crafting, to the extent that she forgets to attend to other activities such as self-care, relationships, and work activities.

In addition to engaging in repetitive behaviors, there is the recurrent theme in autism of doing so without specific meaning and purpose. The ASD individual may lack the ability to differentiate between a meaningful goal-directed activity and a repetitive time-consuming activity that has no purpose. If the individual can identify the difference, she often has difficulty regulating her behavior to focus on meaning and goals rather than repetition.

Patient Scenario: Marta

Marta was a nineteen-year-old university student majoring in art. She had done fairly well in elementary school, but floundered in middle school. Family and teachers were perplexed, and Marta was unable to verbalize the source of her difficulty.

Her parents obtained a full assessment of her thinking skills, academic abilities, and mood. The local psychologist who performed the assessment diagnosed her with autism spectrum disorder. Among other symptoms not highlighted here, she demonstrated uneven cognitive abilities with significantly better spatial than verbal intellectual and memory abilities. Her attention and speed of thought were low average at the best of times, and worse in situations that felt chaotic or required multi-tasking.

One of the intervention strategies to help Marta was to guide her toward subjects that were somewhat focused on spatial abilities (art, geometry) and to add pictures, videos, and demonstrations to subjects like literature, science, and history to help her learn the otherwise verbal information. Some subjects continued to be quite a challenge, but with the support of her school and her parents, she was able to graduate high school and obtain an art scholarship at a local college.

Another helpful intervention involved the use of a supplement to develop a more normalized sleep pattern. Marta found that taking 8 mg of melatonin one hour before bed helped ready her for sleep. She also developed a routine of taking a warm bath with lavender oil 30 minutes before bed, a habit that supported rest and sleep. Having a regular sleep schedule helped her get to class on time and improved her emotional resilience throughout the day.

Marta and her parents learned about the associated features of autism that impacted her daily life in addition to the symptoms used for an actual diagnosis. For Marta, intervention and support in the areas of sleep and cognitive/memory abilities helped her use her strengths to navigate school and achieve greater independence.

Chapter 3

Language and Communication

James was a forty-eight-year-old man with a new diagnosis of autism spectrum disorder. Since the time of his diagnosis, he had gained the support of some community workers and a consistent medical team. In the context of his medical care, it was identified that a significant barrier to health was James's lack of communication with the team. Although he generally answered questions when asked, he never initiated a call to the office when he had concerns, and he never came to his appointments prepared with questions. He never volunteered information about his functioning at home—nutrition and diet, sleep, anxiety, finances—if the topic wasn't first brought up by his team.

As part of his overall care plan, he was assigned a counselor named Mary. One of the first goals of counseling was to improve communication between James and the team. Once James was comfortable talking with Mary, he agreed that he would practice some communication skills with her. The first skill they worked on was his ability to bring something up to the team that wasn't specifically asked.

During the first stage of training, James was taught that all his medical appointments would have the same predictable format. Among other things, there would be a specific time for him to bring up one topic or question. Because James knew this was expected and would be a regular part of his appointments, he and Mary practiced ways for him to identify a topic and begin a conversation when it was his turn to speak.

It became clear that James did best when he was given specific topics as conversation cues. It was identified that he would initiate conversation about sleep, stress levels, or how he felt when he came to a medical appointment.

During his next few medical appointments, this was a very difficult thing for James to adjust to. After brainstorming and practicing with Mary, he was eventually able to initiate his first topic during the third appointment. He chose the topic of sleep, and let his team know that it took him three hours to fall asleep the previous night. Although he wasn't able to elaborate why it had been so difficult to fall asleep, his initiative in communicating this detail was considered a success. Eventually, he made more progress talking to his medical team.

After six months, it was clear that James was sticking to his original three topics, so Mary helped him to choose three additional topics of conversation. As a result, they discovered some important information about his health habits at home, and were able to help him accordingly.

James's story highlights the importance of basic communication skills for navigating everyday life, something that individuals in the autism spectrum struggle with routinely.

Successful communication between two individuals requires an understanding of the words being used, but it also has to do with sentence construction and word order. Someone may exaggerate an opinion or point of view as a way to argue her point or to make a joke. Much of interpersonal communication is peppered with metaphors, similes, and idioms.

Prosody, the emotions within one's voice, as well as facial expressions and gestures, all enhance and define the meaning behind the words. When we're talking to someone, we're often conveying a message behind our words; thus, there is a need to read between the lines, so to speak. We must have the ability to start a conversation, respond to the comments of others, observe social turn taking, and know when the conversation is over.

All of these nuances of interpersonal communication are challenging for those in the autism spectrum. Let's take a closer look at the most common communication challenges for ASD individuals.

Social Approach

Social approach refers to the individual's ability to approach others and begin communicating with them. Individuals with ASD can feel empty when they find someone near them that they should speak to. Coming up with ideas for conversation can be stressful, and conversation starters often feel awkward. Social events that require mingling and small talk may be agonizing.

Conversational Turn Taking and Social Reciprocity

Conversational turn taking has to do with the ability to respond when spoken to and to keep a conversation volleying back and forth like a tennis match. Reciprocity in conversation has to do with how a person's comments impact the turn of the conversation. For example, if I see someone wearing a shirt with a fishing logo on it, and I say, "Oh, I see you like fishing. I love fishing too," the person would know it is her turn to talk, and her comment should include something about fishing. However, if this individual is in the autism spectrum, she might respond with several comments about politics, never approaching the topic of fishing. She lacks the expected ability to build and maintain a conversational topic and transition when a new topic is appropriate. If one of the speakers changes the topic from fishing to childhood memories of a vacation on Lake Michigan, the other speaker knows to transition to topics such as childhood memories, vacations, or Midwest recreational locations. These types of conversational shifts are challenging for ASD individuals.

Reading Other People and Understanding Context

Within the autism spectrum, individuals often have difficulty detecting and adequately responding to the undertones of a conversation. If they are speaking too long about a topic that is not of interest to others, they may fail to detect that they have lost their audience and that others in the group need to switch topics. They may have difficulty reading the body language of those they are speaking to. For instance, they may have challenges determining if the listener is distracted, upset, frustrated, or tired.

It is common for individuals in the autism spectrum to have difficulty mirroring another person's tone or responding in an appropriate way. Examples of this are, "I see that you are really frustrated. What can I do to help?" or "It looks like now is not a good time to talk. How about tomorrow?"

Individuals who struggle with these abilities also may not understand that certain conversations appropriate at a party may not be appropriate at a funeral. For example, the ASD individual may have one conversational topic, such as the Civil War, but not have the ability to change topics to easily match the context of the conversation or discussion.

Speech with Abstract Meaning

Those in the autism spectrum often have difficulty with forms of speech that are not straightforward and concrete in meaning. Below are some examples of figurative speech that can be problematic:

- **Simile**: A comparison between two subjects that are not usually linked: "The man was as brave as a lion in battle."

- **Metaphor**: Two subjects that are not usually linked are described as the same or equal: "The man was a lion in battle."

- **Idiom**: A figurative phrase: "The grass is always greener on the other side."

- **Personification**: A figure of speech in which human qualities are given to an object or animal: "The stars smiled down at us."

- **Rhetorical Question**: A question the listener is not expected to answer: "How does my boss expect me to do the work of two people?"

- **Hyperbole**: Exaggerated statements or claims not meant to be taken literally: "The boat was as fast as lightning."

Translating Meaning: Open-Ended Questions, Concepts, and Constructs

It is also common in the autism spectrum for the individual to have difficulty understanding ideas with abstract content or ✓ varying interpretations.

In the case of open-ended questions, the individual may have difficulty intuiting the speaker's intent. If the speaker says, "Tell me about yourself," the ASD individual can feel a bit lost because there is no clear starting point or structure; these things must be inferred from the context.

For example, if the person asking this question is a hiring manager interviewing the ASD individual for a job, it can be inferred that the speaker is asking for some basic personal history and more in-depth history relating to the job. Once the context is interpreted correctly, the job candidate may state, "Well, I grew up in Chicago but attended university here in town. I have just completed my bachelor's degree in computer science and am very interested in your current opening."

If the speaker is a spouse and asks, "How was your day?" he is looking for interpersonal connection and a sharing of interesting new information. If his wife correctly interprets the context, she will likely describe her excitement about the new job rather than the specific lines of code she programmed that day. However, the individual with autism often has difficulty distinguishing the context of the question and determining how that should impact behavior and communication.

With regard to concepts, the ASD individual may have difficulty understanding instructions such as "Please clean the house while I'm at work today, or "Organize your legal paperwork before we see the lawyer next week." In these instances, the requests are about an idea that could be interpreted differently by different people.

A spouse with autism might feel lost when presented with such vague ideas. He might understand the words being spoken, but not know how to translate them into action. This leads to procrastination and inaction as he struggles with what exactly he is supposed to do.

The neurotypical spouse may come home and feel very frustrated when she discovers that her husband didn't follow through with her request.

There may have been more success, however, if the request was less conceptual and more concrete. As another example, if the couple is planning to have friends over that night, the neurotypical spouse could say, "Ben and Judy are coming for dinner tonight. Before they come, we need to unload the dishwasher, wipe the counters clean, and vacuum the living room rug. Since you'll be home today, can you do those three things while I'm at work?" Because the information in this sentence is specific, there is less chance of a translation problem and more chance of task completion by the ASD listener.

Constructs are similar in that they involve abstract thought and are not tangible, simple, or concrete. Rather, they are ideas or theories formed in the mind, and can mean different things to different people. Constructs include concepts such as freedom, love, success, and trust.

To the extent that two individuals are attempting to communicate but have different understandings of these constructs, there can be tension and misunderstanding, and the sense that they are at cross-purposes with one another in conversation.

For example, if the neurotypical individual asks the ASD individual for more freedom or more love, this may be as confusing as asking a neurotypical individual for more "purple" or more "flat." The individual with autism may not be able to successfully and easily translate requests from others that involve constructs.

Understanding the Main Idea

For the individual with ASD traits, the ability to capture the most important part of the conversation may be quite difficult. The neurotypical listener may be able to understand the main idea, even in the midst of other comments or details, whereas the ASD individual may catch a detail but miss the main idea. He may recall that the room was very bright and the speaker was talking loudly and quickly. Perhaps he recalls that there was an interruption to the conversation when the speaker accepted a phone call.

Or, after a meeting with the boss, he recalls that his boss talked about his previous project and his new project, but the boss leaves knowing that their conversation was about the need for staff to complete the new project more quickly than the old project was completed. The ASD individual may leave with the knowledge that his boss is aware of both projects and that the first one is completed. He knows that he should proceed with the new project, but he doesn't understand that the priority for the new project is speed, not accuracy.

Nonverbal Communication

- **Faces:** The human face is one of the most difficult constellations of visual input our brain has to process. There are a multitude of nuances depending on the light/shadows, distance of the person that is being seen, and tilt of the head. Facial expressions and movements also add to the complexity.

Individuals with autism have difficulty processing faces and expressions as a complete entity. The eyes are sometimes emphasized as being particularly hard to interpret, and sometimes are visually overwhelming to individuals in the spectrum. These individuals may also have a hard time recognizing familiar people when viewing them from distances and angles. Some report that they recognize an individual by her eyeglasses or haircut. This may add to the rigidity of reactions when a person with ASD becomes upset that someone else has changed their look. Additionally, ASD individuals can have problems identifying gender if a stereotypical look is not maintained, such as if a man has long hair.

One of my patients tends to recognize the people he knows by what they wear frequently. He assumes that is how it is for everyone. He explained his confusion during one encounter with friends by saying, "I don't know how they recognized me. I wore my new coat, and they have never seen that coat before."

- **Voice**: Individuals with autism often have difficulty with the rhythm and flow of speech. Some have problems communicating emotions through their voice (prosody), and/or they have difficulty understanding the vocal emotions of others. If an individual with autistic qualities is asked to say the same sentence, first in a happy voice and then in an angry or a sarcastic voice, he may struggle with any true contrast in his prosody. Additionally, many ASD individuals speak very quickly using lots of words, whereas the norm would be a more regulated rate of speech and fewer words. Some may have a consistently heightened and happy tone to their voice compared to the more flat tone of others with autism.

- **Gestures**: There is often a range of deficit regarding the use and comprehension of gestures. The ASD individual may not adequately use gestures to clarify what s/he is saying, or the gestures might be somewhat less meaningful or connected to the topic and flow of conversation. Additionally, as with other symptoms, the gestures may seem forced rather than spontaneous. For example, someone may use two gestures repeatedly and compulsively rather than the more typical variety of gestures to emphasize what s/he is saying. Many individuals in the spectrum use simple gestures such as waving hello, but are unable to communicate more complex ideas, such as gesturing that it is time to leave or to stop talking.

- **Postures**: There is evidence of differences in gait (walking), movement patterns, and postural control in the autism spectrum. One may notice that an individual in the spectrum has a rigid posture or a posture that does not clearly communicate how the person feels, such as a slumped posture when fatigued or a more in-drawn, hunched posture when uncomfortable.

- **Personal Space**: Those with spectrum characteristics often have difficulties understanding and navigating personal boundaries during close communication. This may occur at either end of the continuum. For instance, an individual may invade the space of others without an awareness of how his presence impacts them. In contrast, he may feel uncomfortable with physical closeness or gestures involving touch during communication. He may back away from someone who leans toward him while speaking of important issues. He may avoid standing in lines where he will be in close proximity to others.

Each of these verbal and nonverbal differences in communication can impact many areas of life including the ability to communicate to a teacher about academic difficulty, to a spouse about household and family responsibilities, or to a doctor about medical instructions and general health recommendations.

Training in social skills is recognized as an evidence-based intervention for those with autism spectrum disorder. Social skills are usually picked up instinctively by the general population, but individuals in the autism spectrum often need specific training about what is important when talking to other people. The training can be performed individually or within a group setting in which specific skills are taught, modeled, practiced, and reinforced. The goal is for the participants to understand that these skills can be generalized to other settings even if those settings are not practiced with the trainer.

For example, the individual can start by learning about social approach. Then he can practice social approach in his own environment. He can memorize idioms so that he can understand what people are referring to in conversation when they use them.

Next, the lesson may be about the role of hyperbole in humor. For example, the ASD individual may need to learn that extremes can be humorous. Examples can be practiced with the trainer: "I just bought so many groceries that I won't ever have to shop again!" The learner is taught that the speaker knows the statement isn't true, but is trying to convey how much shopping she did by exaggerating and thus making the story humorous.

Social skills training may take place in the context of counseling. At other times, a community program may run a social skills group. The group can be geared toward the specific needs of the participants. If adults are attending, the skills taught should be ones the participants will use and practice on a daily basis, such as communicating with family or speaking to a coworker. They should be appropriate for the intellectual and language abilities of the participants.

Chapter 4

Executive Function

Mrs. Allen was a fifty-eight-year-old woman who brought her husband of twelve years to our office for counseling. Mr. Allen was a <u>seventy-two-year-old</u> former mechanical engineer who had been retired from his job for the past four years.

His wife was energetic and social, animated in her descriptions, and ready to get to the bottom of her husband's change in activity level. Mr. Allen was more taciturn, and he appeared content to be led by his forceful partner. Indeed, his passivity was one of Mrs. Allen's concerns. She loved his willingness to follow her on her travels and to try foods from all varieties of international cuisine, but she now felt he was almost <u>too compliant</u> and easy-going, as if <u>he had no interest in anything</u>.

Since his retirement, he seemed perfectly willing to sit in his chair or putter around the house. During his career, he had been a brilliant engineer. He had multiple patents and was a whiz at math. Now, he appeared content to be <u>still, without direction or goals</u>. Although Mr. Allen denied sadness, regret, or anxiety, his wife wondered if he might be depressed. Although her reasoning appeared logical, was depression really the root of her husband's change in behavior?

Autism spectrum disorder is often overlooked in individuals with average or advanced intellectual abilities, particularly in older adults who may have completed many seasons of life undiagnosed.

One of the brain's abilities is called executive function (EF), a cognitive ability that is impacted by the connections in the center front of the brain. This ability is completely separate from one's intellect.

Executive function can be negatively affected by quite a few medical issues, including traumatic brain injury, stroke, and infection. It can also be affected by developmental conditions. In fact, attention deficit disorder is actually a disorder of executive function. EF is often one of the biggest culprits in the daily struggles of individuals with ASD.

I often think of executive function as a symphony conductor. When the conductor is skilled and proficient, each instrument in the orchestra performs smoothly in concert with the others. The music is lyrical and flowing, the perfect counterbalance between intensity and calm. Without a conductor, the instruments, although perhaps played well individually, would make a clashing and disjointed sound with no coherent melody and no cohesive message that speaks to the souls of the listeners.

In the same way, an individual who has strong thinking skills— word knowledge, spatial reasoning, verbal problem solving abilities—but who has impaired executive function struggles to use his thinking skills in a coordinated and efficient manner for daily activities. This is because the brain's executive function is in charge of bringing the base cognitive skills together to produce a melodic flow at school, at work, and at home.

Executive function can be very difficult to explain and includes many sub-skills. I prefer to use the breakdown and definitions presented by Peg Dawson and Richard Guare in their *Smart but Scattered* series. The authors point out that every neurotypical person in the general population has a pattern of strengths and weaknesses within the more specific sub-skills of executive function. However, individuals with developmental conditions such as ADD or ASD, or those with brain injury or neurodegenerative conditions, typically have more significant and pervasive difficulty.

Let's look at the sub-skills within executive function.

Time Management

Time is a concept that our brain has to learn to internalize. We must get a sense of how ten minutes feels different from forty-five minutes. For some, the internalization of time isn't easy, and can lead to quite a struggle. Although chronic lateness is often a problem, some individuals are chronically early. Individuals who have difficulty with time management typically struggle with appointments and deadlines, but also with estimating how long it will take to complete a task. It is, therefore, challenging to adjust their routine to complete a new task.

For some who have difficulties in this area, a visual timer can be a significant help. Time Timers® are an option often used. These timers have a large white face with a red panel that can be pulled to cover a certain amount of time on a clock face. As time elapses, so does the red color. It can be particularly helpful for any individual who has trouble transitioning from one task to another. The disappearing red can help this person mentally prepare for an upcoming change in task.

Another way to build this skill is to have the individual time himself as he completes certain activities. He should do this for several days to determine a pattern. Once he knows that his typical shower takes ten to thirteen minutes, he can build this into his morning routine. In another example, to help an ASD individual determine how long it takes to drive from one location to another, she can set the GPS device when she leaves one location, and make a note of the number of minutes it estimates the trip will take. If she doesn't have a GPS or a car with this software built in, she can input the two locations on Google Maps or other online map software. This will show the estimated driving time when the option for Directions is chosen.

Patient Scenario: Michael

Michael had trouble arriving to classes and activities on time during his school years. He always felt distracted and behind. When he began his first adult job at a library, he and his job coach knew that punctuality would be important. Michael used a Time Timer® in the morning to keep him on track. He set fifteen minutes for his shower and dressing routine, twenty minutes to pack his lunch and gather his materials for work, and ten minutes to eat a snack bar and drink some water. He knew from timing his drive to work that in good weather the trip generally took between eighteen and twenty-two minutes. After six months, he found he could set the timer for forty-five minutes at the beginning of his routine, and stay on track for leaving the house thirty minutes before his day started at work. Additionally, because he wasn't leaving the house too late, he wasn't speeding on the way to the library. He reached a personal financial goal of avoiding a speeding ticket for the entirety of his first year at work.

Behavioral Initiation

The center and front of the brain is what turns on and off our behavior. You can think of the brain as having a gas pedal and a brake pedal like a car. Although motivation and effort are important for behavior, our brain needs to say "Go" to a certain behavior to get us moving. Many individuals with executive function problems have trouble starting an activity, particularly if it is a multi-step project or an activity that is frequent and mundane, such as laundry. One can see how time management problems and difficulties starting certain behaviors can feed procrastination. An individual with these challenges often needs reminders to start a task, and when completed, to continue with the next task.

Individuals with difficulties initiating behaviors often benefit from determining the types of tasks that are hard to start. Some of the tasks may be too large in scope, and therefore feel overwhelming. In these circumstances, teach the individual to break down the task into smaller, more achievable steps. For example, if the boss requires the ASD individual to present key elements of the new computer system to the team in four days, perhaps the small step of writing a list of four advantages of the new system would be a good first step. If another individual has a goal of selling his home and moving to a retirement apartment, cleaning the garage may be too overwhelming a goal to start. Perhaps the first goal could be to clear out specific items first. For instance, he could take the electronics, paints, and pesticides to a recycling center.

Other tasks may be so boring and uninteresting that they do not compel the person to start the activity. This can be true of activities that are repetitive and simple, but that must be done as a regular part of daily living, such as washing the dishes and putting away folded clothes. In these circumstances, the individual can find a way to add fun to the boring task. For example, she could build in a game to beat her previous time spent unloading the dishwasher. Perhaps she could listen to her favorite music while scrubbing the bathtub, making this otherwise dreaded task a bit more invigorating. Other times, having a reward at the end of the task is successful. For example, if the person is wild about reading or video games or history, she can promise herself the reward of doing more of her favorite activity after she completes a mundane task.

A third recommendation is to avoid open-ended tasks. Individuals in the autism spectrum often have difficulty translating a huge unspecified task into several smaller specified tasks. For example, depending on the individual, "clean the kitchen," "be polite," or "present on any topic of interest to your team" feels vague and enormous in scope. There are so many versions of what each of those tasks could look like that it doesn't take true form in his mind. This individual may know that he does best when given specific input. For example, his spouse may post an instruction sheet for what "clean the kitchen" means: put food away, wipe the counters, and sweep the floor. His mother may explain that being polite in this situation means that when he receives a gift from someone, he should thank the person even if he doesn't like the gift. His boss may provide more structure in his assignment, such as, "Your presentation can be on the topic of how to make a syllabus or how to write IEP goals."

Patient Scenario: Alice

Alice was a forty-five-year-old woman in the autism spectrum who worked part time at a flower shop and lived alone in an apartment. Although she was very particular about which direction her toothbrush was facing in the bathroom and the symmetry of her chair against the wall in the living room, she was very disorganized about the general cleanliness of her apartment. Her niece had talked to her multiple times about responsibility, germs, and the importance of doing basic household chores. However, talking and reasoning did nothing to improve the behavior. With coaching from a community mentor, Alice's niece was able to make a simple schedule for Alice to follow at home. Each day, Alice only needed to complete one small task such as wipe the kitchen counter or put her clean clothes away. Each time Alice completed the household task as scheduled, her niece brought over a new and unusual bead for Alice's craft collection. Over time, Alice was able to do more than one task a day as long as rewards were present and tasks were clearly defined, specific, and brief.

Prioritization and Planning

Individuals with ASD often have difficulty conceptualizing and completing long-term goals and outcomes. They may have significant problems knowing where to start and what to do after the first step is completed. They often have great difficulty identifying the most important part of the task, the one that should take priority in terms of time, energy, and attention.

One issue in the spectrum that interferes with prioritization is the unusual lens through which the individual views and interprets her world. Individuals with ASD qualities often associate deep meaning and importance to things that others would not consider important. For example, one person in the spectrum may prioritize steps to organizing his apartment by emphasizing the need for all of the items on the fireplace mantel to be red. Another may feel that making sure she has food items in quantities that are odd numbers is very important.

This tendency to focus on aspects of the environment that neurotypical individuals don't notice or consider important is common in the spectrum. Sometimes the small details are of great significance to the ASD individual, but there is a lack of appreciation and emphasis on the bigger more meaningful picture. In these circumstances, the individual may need outside structure from a mentor, friend, or family member to ensure that the most important needs are met, such as health, safety, and hygiene.

Another barrier to prioritizing has to do with the issue of sequencing. Sequencing is an executive function skill that involves thinking about multiple options—objects, choices, individuals—and considering which should rank first, second, third, and so on. For example, once it is established that cleaning the kitchen means sweeping the floor, wiping the counters, and putting the food away, the person needs to figure out which task to do first, then second, then third. He needs to sequence his options and prioritize them in a certain order. Although neurotypical individuals can do this without thinking, such as knowing to put the food away first so that it does not sit out and spoil, it may take time and energy for an individual in the autism spectrum to sequence and rank his options.

The ASD individual also might not understand that she cannot sufficiently clean the counters while the food is still sitting out and cluttering those counters. Therefore, she needs guidance in understanding the meaning and significance of each step, and conceptualizing how it affects the other steps in the process of task completion.

Some individuals in the spectrum may be able to sequence two or three steps or choices, but may become overwhelmed with a longer list of choices, such as knowing which step to do first in a ten-step task, or deciding which movie to see at a seven-screen theatre. Additionally, many individuals in the autism spectrum get stuck on certain sequences when carrying out their daily activities. One person, for example, may feel it is very important to read the paper before she leaves for work even if she is running late. Another may become upset if he cannot drink his coffee before eating his sausage. This is typical of executive function in ASD individuals. For instance, the individual may show too much adherence to detail in certain activities (needing to drink coffee before eating sausage) while showing too little adherence to detail in other activities (dirty clothes and garbage littering the floor). This imbalance is often detrimental to the individual and confusing to those around him.

Planning requires multiple skills, including the ability to break large tasks into smaller tasks, estimating how long a specific small task will take, and deciding how to pace the tasks to meet a deadline. The ASD individual needs to use prioritization strategies to determine which steps should occur first, next, and last. Individuals in the autistic spectrum tend to struggle with this aspect of pulling all the pieces together. Often, they benefit from having someone teach them strategies for achieving goals and making plans.

An additional aspect of the spectrum that leads to planning difficulty is concrete thinking. Individuals with ASD often have trouble considering possibilities that have not occurred yet. Instead, they get stuck on what has already occurred. Because of this, they have trouble generalizing from previous experiences to predict future outcomes. For example, a neurotypical individual might say, "I enjoyed teaching Sunday school, so I might enjoy being a teacher." An individual with autism might say, "Well, I don't know if I would like classroom teaching. How could I know that? I'm not a teacher."

Here is an excerpt from my visit with Beth, a twenty-six-year-old young woman in the autism spectrum:

> **Dr. Regan**: Beth, I'm going to ask you how you might feel in certain situations that you have not experienced. How do you think you would feel if you went to the moon?
>
> **Beth**: That would be an overwhelming concept. I don't know how rational that is.

Dr. R: How do you think you would feel if you came in tenth place in an Olympic swimming race?

Beth: That's a good question. I can't swim fast.

Dr. R: What are your goals, Beth? What would you like to have happen in your life?

Beth: I love France. I collect books and pictures about France. I would like to move to France and guard the Eiffel Tower.

Dr. R: How do you plan to reach that goal?

Beth: Not sure.

Individuals in the autism spectrum are also likely to have trouble planning for contingencies. A neurotypical wedding planner, for example, would have the ability to plan an outdoor wedding with all possible weather outcomes accounted for. An individual in the autism spectrum would struggle to plan for theoretical outcomes.

Organization

This refers to a person's ability to create systems to track information and materials. A person with fully developed organizational strength may use lists, planners, calendars, bins with labels, and hooks for coats, aprons, and sports equipment. A person who struggles with organization may rely on his own mental tracking of where things are rather than specific strategies and tools to keep things in place and on track. He may have multiple piles of things in several areas, each in different stages of completion. These individuals often say they have "lost track" of where they put that sticky note, bill, or letter from the teacher.

Individuals in the spectrum often have uneven organization. They may show extreme and rigid organization within certain areas of particular interest to them while showing significant and chronic disorganization in other areas of life. For example, Gwen's map collection always stays in the far left corner of the living room, and the vacuum cleaner always stays in the downstairs closet toward the right, but she has multiple piles of dirty and clean laundry on the floor that she never puts away or separates. Phil has stacks of magazines, bills, letters, and newspapers on the kitchen table in no apparent order, but his model ship collection is perfectly aligned on the mantel, each an inch from the one next to it and two inches from the edge, all dusted regularly and put back exactly in place.

Organization involves strategies and plans. Some individuals with ASD are able to learn strategies and use them independently. Others respond quite well when someone organizes their space for them and teaches them how to use organizational tools, such as labeling a shelf BOOKS and labeling a bin BILLS. Some prefer pictures for labels instead of words. Still other individuals lack the ability to show much progress toward independent use of strategy, and may instead need a person who can regularly cue them: "This is a book. It goes here."

Patient Scenario: Christopher

Christopher was a seventy-year-old gentleman who was retired from his job as a research scientist. He had never married nor had children, but his niece was attentive to his needs and health. He kept his kitchen pantry particularly organized with cans of food in symmetric rows and labels facing in the same direction. The cans were alphabetical according to content. He paid his bills on time, and he meticulously balanced his checkbook, sometimes taking as many as four hours to account for a discrepancy of a few pennies.

60

Of particular concern, however, was his office, cluttered with multiple piles of varying heights of scientific journal articles, charts, graphs, and statistics. Because the piles covered multiple surfaces including the floor, he had slipped a few times on stray papers. When he recently searched for his will and other legal documents, he was unable to find them in the clutter.

Christopher's niece was able to help him by putting all his legal documents into a small filing cabinet in the far corner. She also purchased and labeled storage cubbies for his journal articles. Some of the cubbies were mounted on the wall, and others were stacked on the floor on a series of narrow throw rugs.

Christopher knew he was allowed to put articles in the cubbies or on the throw rugs, but not directly on the wood floor, because that was where he walked.

This technique gave him a visually defined space so that he could continue to put things on the floor, which he tended to do anyway, as long as he stacked them on the throw rugs. This kept the piles from spilling over into his walking area. He used this visual cue to improve his organizational skills and his safety.

Response Inhibition

Response inhibition refers to the ability to restrain oneself from an action until it can be considered with care. It includes the ability to delay a choice until certain factors are in place. The front part of the brain is supposed to act as a filter that keeps certain things "inside" our heads and allows other things to come "out" as actions. In those with impaired response inhibition, the filter does not function adequately. Individuals with difficulty in this area often do or say things without thinking about the consequences or risks.

The lack of filtering common in an ASD individual can have significant consequences. For example, she may blurt out impulsively during a work meeting and evaluate a client in a way that jeopardizes the company's goals and her relationship with her employers. He may use his disability check to buy books about trains rather than using the money to pay his telephone bill. Anything that is said or done without pausing to consider possible outcomes is considered impulsive and disinhibited.

Patient Scenario: Julia

Julia was a forty-two-year-old lawyer whose firm served a large corporation in the city. Julia was a competent attorney whose strengths served her well in her career—her persistence, her passion for getting things right, and her ability to recall obscure legal precedents that rivaled a computer search engine. However, she had been disciplined at work for "telling it like it is" in a blunt fashion without taking into consideration others' viewpoints, and for doing so in front of clients or public figures.

She was working with a counselor to enhance her people skills so that she could achieve her work goals. Julia and her counselor both agreed that her lack of filter and her difficulty in restraining her comments was holding her back at work. They decided to establish prompts to make her more aware of what she was about to say so that she could pause before speaking.

Julia purchased a new bracelet that had a round opal in the center. She trained herself to recognize the urge to speak that welled up inside her when discussing a volatile topic at work. When she felt the urgency build, she twirled the opal five times before she spoke. This deliberate pause helped her to think about the potential consequences of what she was about to say. Julia also asked her boss to give her a signal if she was overstepping in her comments to clients. They decided the signal would be an ear tug, a discreet reminder that she should count to five and consider the consequences of her words before speaking. As time went on, Julia's boss had to use the ear tug less often, though Julia stuck to the strategy of twirling her bracelet before speaking. Both she and her boss were pleased with her progress.

Patient Scenario: Charles

Charles was a twenty-four-year-old young man with an intellectual disability and autism spectrum behaviors. He worked part time as a janitor in a workshop setting, initially set up with the assistance of a job coach. A payee organized his money, and an aide taught him money management skills to improve his financial independence.

Charles loved historical and modern trains. Whenever he was given an allowance to pay his bills, he was tempted to spend the money immediately on train collectibles and books. This urgency decreased his ability to stop and think about what bills must be paid first.

The strategy that worked best was to teach Charles to put his allowance money in a basket with two sections. The money was placed in the first section in a large envelope with a big red STOP sign on the front. The sign was something Charles knew about from riding the bus. It cued him to STOP and check the second section of the basket, which contained his bills for the month.

If the second section was empty, he knew he had paid his bills and could use the rest of the monthly allowance on trains. If the section contained a bill, he must pay the bill before spending the money. The easily identifiable STOP sign helped him to pause and think before acting on his initial strong impulse.

Working Memory

Working memory is actually a form of attention. You use this skill when you mentally track information in your mind as you complete a task with several steps. It may involve using the knowledge you've gained from a previous task to accomplish a new task. Working memory is the ability to keep things in mind while completing an action.

An individual with ASD may have problems with efficient working memory. For example, he may have trouble getting out of the house in the morning with everything he needs for work—wallet, keys, phone, briefcase, lunch bag, umbrella. He may lose track of deadlines for projects or forget to lock his file cabinet before he leaves work. Another individual may have problems keeping in mind instructions from her boss while she completes a project.

For those who have problems keeping things in mind while working, they may wish to have written or recorded cues to help them stay on track. The individual who likes technology may use his smart phone recorder to keep track of ideas, lists of things to do, or the steps required to complete a task. This is a tech version of the small pocket notebooks that another individual might prefer for jotting a few notes throughout the day. There is also a phone app that allows a person to verbally put something on a list by speaking into the phone. The phone transcribes the verbal instruction onto a written list that is viewable on the phone screen.

Others may prefer picture cues or written reminders. An ASD individual who goes to the grocery store with the assistance of an aide may bring pictures of the foods she needs, putting each picture in her purse when she puts the food in her basket. Another individual may lose track of what he has completed in his bedtime routine and what he still needs to do. For this individual, a written list taped to the bathroom mirror might be helpful.

If he needs the physical activity of checking off each task as he completes it, he could keep a small whiteboard with a marker in the bathroom, and erase the check marks each morning to have a clean slate for the next bedtime routine. Alternatively, he could have small laminated pictures of each part of his routine that he turns over when each task has been completed. No matter which method is used, these tasks could include 1) take off clothes and put in hamper or laundry basket, 2) put on pajamas, 3) brush teeth, 4) wash face, and 5) place towel on the towel bar (if removed to dry face and hands).

Cues can also be placed in specific and relevant locations. For example, if the individual needs to make sure she attends to four things every time she leaves the house, a sign can be placed on the inside of the front door to cue her attention to these things before leaving the house: turn off lights, turn off stove, adjust the thermostat, and lock the doors.

Another example might be to have the individual put items together the night before that must be taken when she leaves in the morning. If remembering to take a lunch to work is a problem, perhaps putting the car keys in the fridge next to the lunch bag will work, coupled with a sign on the inside front door that reads "Get your lunch and your car keys out of the fridge." She can't leave without her keys, and this will also remind her to grab her lunch.

To keep in mind possible changes to the driving route, such as road construction and resulting detours, or remembering where he needs to stop on the way home from work to run a few errands, the individual could write cues on masking tape and stick those to the steering wheel the night before so that he doesn't have to remember to do this extra task during the morning rush to get ready and out of the house on time.

Patient Scenario: James

James worked as a data entry clerk. His job was predictable for the most part, but sometimes there were schedule changes due to meetings or varied completion dates for larger projects. Although he tried to use basic strategies to stay on track, such as keeping his calendar up to date, he often found himself losing track of his tasks and materials. Two of his biggest difficulties were leaving home without everything he needed for work, and leaving work without locking and securing his materials.

His friend helped him devise a strategy whereby he made one laminated card for each day of the week. Before he left for work on Monday, he looked at the Monday card and saw that he needed to bring a lunch because every Monday he attended a lunch-and-learn meeting at noon. The card also reminded him of the things he needed to take with him every day—glasses, keys, phone, wallet, and briefcase.

His Tuesday card let him know that he went straight to the gym after work for his karate class and needed to take his gym bag as well as his usual materials for work. Likewise, he used one card to cue him to lock his file cabinet, shut down his computer, and check his calendar for the next day before leaving work. Because his end-of-day card stayed the same, he eventually replaced it with one that had the words "three things" written on it as a visual cue. He practiced remembering the three things on his own. Eventually, he was able to stop using a cue for his end-of-day routine, but continued using his morning cards to keep him on track with his changing daily schedules.

Sustained Attention

An individual demonstrates sustained attention when he remains focused on a task even if it is boring or routine, or if he is feeling tired or distractible.

Someone who daydreams or frequently switches activities has problems with sustained attention and keeping his behavior on target. He may rush through a task or give up quickly in order to move on to another task. He may frequently ask when the task will be over, or make off-topic comments during the task.

One strategy for improving attention to a task or goal is to break the job into smaller components that are more reasonably attended to. For example, instead of sitting down to pay seven bills, someone may choose to pay three bills and take a fifteen-minute break. If the person is physically able, it is helpful to do simple repetitive tasks such as vacuuming, pulling weeds, or starting a load of laundry as a way to take a break from tasks that involve a heavy dose of thinking skills.

Some individuals are able to stay more focused on a task if they have background noise, like doing their computer work at a coffee shop or listening to music, whereas others are distracted by noise. Individuals who stay focused with noise may choose to play background music, perhaps without lyrics, such as instrumental music, or to listen to recordings of nature sounds. I have even worked with individuals who feel most focused when playing a metronome in the background. For this, they typically use metronome apps, and set the tick-tock sound at whatever interval gives them optimal focus.

Seating and positioning can also impact attention and goal-directed thought for some. I have worked with individuals in the spectrum who feel much more focused when lying on their stomach on the floor to read, write, or to use their laptop. Others prefer to straddle a chair while working at a table. Even others have a strategy of wrapping a resistance exercise band around the four legs of their chair and pushing the band with their legs or feet while working. Chewing gum can also help some individuals focus on a brain-intensive task.

For an individual who must sit in a class or a conference meeting for an extended period, there will be limitations to her ability to shorten the task, add fun, or take breaks. One option is to make sure she takes a break before the meeting. A walking or movement break can be particularly effective. She can squeeze a stress ball during the meeting to provide some sensory input to keep her alert and focused. (We will discuss this in greater depth in the sensory chapter).

Patient Scenario: Celeste

Celeste was a twenty-year-old young woman taking an algebra class at her local community college. She typically studied two or three hours a day, but wasn't accomplishing much. Her homework was often partially completed, and her exam scores were below what she needed to pass the class. She just couldn't handle the thought of adding more time to her study commitment for this one class. Once she started working with a tutor, it became apparent that she primarily spent time trying to bring her concentration back to the material. Her mind wandered easily, and at the end of the study session, she hadn't accomplished her goals. Her tutor suggested studying less but with more focus.

Celeste learned to set her timer for fifteen minutes and to focus as intently as she could during that time. At the end of the fifteen minutes, she walked her dog around the neighborhood twice. Then, she worked intently for another fifteen minutes. During her break, she allowed herself to get on social media and catch up with her friends for fifteen minutes, and then it was back to math. Although she still spent two or three hours of time in her homework routine, only half was actually spent getting the academic work done, and the other half was spent on physical activity, chores, and fun activities. This technique was more effective, satisfying, and sustainable for Celeste. This new strategy, in combination with tutoring, helped her pass the class.

Metacognition

Individuals with difficulties in the area of metacognition have a hard time evaluating their abilities and performance. This involves asking questions such as "How did I do?" "What am I good at?" and "What goals should I be working toward?" They also have difficulty figuring out what they know and what they don't know. For example, they are likely to give up on a task too soon, stating, "I don't know this" or "I can't do this" rather than encouraging themselves by thinking *I haven't seen this problem before, but I solved a similar one last week. I can get this if I just keep at it.*

Individuals with autism often benefit from reminders to think about how they solved a certain problem, what their process was, and what other strategies might be used to reach the outcome. In the same way that improving time-management skills can involve timing yourself on a task and learning that you take twenty minutes to complete it, metacognitive skills can involve evaluating the quality and process of your work.

Some individuals benefit from evaluating their work alongside a checklist of what good work looks like. An individual who is learning skills related to construction may be given a checklist of what a thorough painting job looks like. He can then look at his work and compare it with the checklist to evaluate his work correctly:

- Did he do a thorough job?
- Did he miss any spots?
- Did he paint only the areas designated, or did he paint over other sections by mistake?
- Did he clean his brushes, rollers, and paint trays when he was finished for the day?
- Did he close the paint cans tightly and put them away?

An individual can also learn self-talk to develop strategies for taking a bird's-eye view of her situation. Instead of getting stuck in a problem or detail, she can be coached to look at bigger and broader issues.

As Dawson and Guare suggest, an individual can ask, "What is my goal? What is my plan to accomplish my goal? Am I following my plan? How did the plan work? Do I need to change a part of the plan to make it more doable?" Using this guidance, an individual seeking to stay on track with bill paying could use cue cards with these questions written on them (one question per card) to guide her thought process and help her stay focused on attaining her goal.

Goal-Directed Persistence

Goal-directed persistence refers to the ability to finish a task before moving on to another. For an individual in the autism spectrum, the ability to give up short-term pleasures for long-term goals can be more challenging than it is for neurotypical individuals. He may start many things but finish few. Likewise, he may give up when things are difficult or when they seem unrelated to his ultimate interests and goals.

Achieving adult goals often involves doing many challenging things until we get to the expected outcome. The delay between finishing one task and achieving the ultimate goal may be weeks, years, or decades. Some goals may never be attained.

Individuals with ASD may struggle with goal-directed persistence for a variety of reasons. They often have problems with metacognitive skills as discussed above, leading them to set goals that are not realistic. For example, an individual with autism who has a fixated interest on food-related topics may have a goal of becoming a famous chef on television. He may show poor persistence in achieving ability-appropriate goals, such as mastering basic math, while focusing entirely on tasks he perceives to be related to his goal of becoming a cooking personality on television, such as watching cooking programs six hours a day. Individuals in the spectrum with low goal-directed persistence often need help setting appropriate goals and taking practical steps to accomplish them.

Because of meta-cognitive difficulties, individuals in the spectrum may develop unrealistic life goals. An intense focus on the identified life goal may mean that the individual lacks a persistent focus on more attainable and immediate goals. The most fruitful outcome is reached when helpers and educators link the individual's interests and strengths to attainable goals.

In addition to the barrier of limited metacognitive skills, our cultural assumption that "you can be whatever you want to be if you work hard enough" can leave people stuck with goals that are not attainable. Although this catchphrase is meant to be motivational, it isn't true. An individual with a moderate intellectual disability is not going to be able to function as Secretary of State no matter how hard he or she tries. A better approach would be for educators to help their students learn strategies to reach achievable goals tailored to their unique abilities.

Once an appropriate long-term goal is determined, the larger goals need to be broken down into multiple smaller and more immediate goals. In order to encourage persistence in working toward a goal, the identified goal must be visible and attainable. Once an individual encounters a task that he is unable to achieve, persistence weakens, and he gives up too soon. When that happens, goals are lost. Each small part of the goal should be achievable for the individual with only intermittent help from others.

Another way to encourage individuals in the autism spectrum to persist with a task is to integrate topics that interest them. One of the prominent features of ASD is a very fixed interest in a few topics. Although the topics may change over time, the interest can be all encompassing, allowing little attention for anything else. If the relevant and meaningful goals that the individual must achieve can include these special-interest topics, the individual will find it easier to complete the task.

If the individual you are working with tends to complete tasks quickly in a slipshod manner rather than persisting to attain accuracy, you may consider setting a timer for the task. Let's assume the individual typically persists at the task for ten minutes then gets distracted and loses interest. Try setting a time of fifteen minutes during which he must continue working even if he has finished. If he completes the task early, he should check his work. By removing the seemingly positive outcome of finishing the task as quickly as possible, the individual may pace himself more appropriately and tolerate small increases in persistence over time.

Patient Scenario: Sherri

Sherri was a sixteen-year-old student with a strong fixated interest in the space program. Her life goal was to become an astronaut, and her favorite activity was to watch Internet videos of shuttle launches. Although she had no identifiable learning disabilities, it was difficult to find ways to engage her in academics. She complained that she did not need to read literature or dissect a frog to be an astronaut. Her parents and educators were concerned that her behavior was closing doors to the most meaningful goals she could reach in her community.

Using Sherri's interest in space as a foundation, they focused on integrating space-related topics into her regular curriculum. For example, in English Composition, she was asked to write a creative short story about space. In her mathematics courses, she was given story problems involving the radii of planets, light refraction in telescopes, and the impact of gravity on speed as the shuttle re-enters the earth's gravitational field. She was allowed to focus on physics and astronomy in her science classes, and she wrote an excellent report on biology experiments completed in space.

The second step was to translate her interest in space into work within the community. Rather than focusing only on being an astronaut, she was able to identify three jobs in her community that involved the topic of space: night janitor at the observatory, courier for delivering community fliers about museum programs to local businesses, and part-time librarian at a planetarium.

Once her participation in appropriate academics improved, and she had some work experience under her belt, her advisors and parents helped her consider possible future museum jobs, such as keeping records of museum objects, leading educational programs for the community, or giving museum tours.

Sherri's academic advisors helped her to identify the coursework she needed to pass in order to work at each of these jobs in a space-related museum setting. They also helped her to locate museums that might have programs of interest. In addition, she committed to community volunteer work as a way of developing independent skills and demonstrating her commitment to space-related topics at schools, museums, and libraries.

Flexibility

One of the most challenging areas within the autism spectrum is flexibility of thought (opinions, facts, strategies for problem solving) and behavior (routines, schedules, routes for travel). Flexibility refers to the ability to adapt to change, consider multiple sources of input, and revise plans based on unexpected obstacles. Generally, those in the spectrum prefer repetition and predictability in life. This preference can manifest in a variety of ways.

- Although Roger's wife suggests several new options, he prefers to watch the same movie multiple times a week.

- Carl has a strict morning routine and insists he must do everything in a specific order.

- Many feel that Joan is a know-it-all because she insists she is right even when shown contrary evidence.

- George was injured in a car accident because he stopped his car and put it in reverse to drive backward after taking the wrong exit on the freeway. He considered this a reasonable decision so that he could find the correct exit rather than driving through town to get back onto the freeway.

- Phil watches only recorded baseball programs so that he can hear the final score before watching the game, thereby avoiding the stress of unexpected outcomes.

Those with ASD often have trouble generating multiple ideas, such as solutions to a problem, topics for a paper, or ideas for a story. They can become stuck on one thought, one outcome, or one solution. They sometimes think in concrete categories such as good or bad, right or wrong, winner or loser. Seeing the complexity of a person or situation may be challenging for them.

Individuals in the spectrum may avoid activities with unknown outcomes, such as games, sporting events, and competitions with winners and losers. Other people may consider the autistic individual to be a sore loser, although the base of her struggle may have more to do with how she handles unexpected events and adjusts to unpredictable outcomes than how she feels about being the winner.

Repetition and adherence to routine can become problematic when changes occur without warning. A detour that takes someone off his typical route to the doctor's office heightens his stress level. Having to buy an alternate brand of toothpaste when the store is out of her preferred brand creates anxiety.

Individuals in the spectrum often benefit from structure and predictability. Having a routine is generally calming and helpful to reduce stress. One of the difficult things about retirement can be the loss of predictability that a job brought to one's daily schedule. The individual wakes up and feels the long unfilled hours of the day bearing down on him, pressuring him to fill them with meaningful activities.

A routine can help with adjustment after retirement. For example, each Monday's routine may include gardening and volunteer work at the Children's Home. Tuesday may be the day for laundry and book club, and so on. This type of structure enhances motivation and initiative because it provides the individual with a comforting sense of calm, regularity, and control over the outcomes of his or her daily life.

Routines for transition can also be helpful. If Pamela finds her husband's frequent absences on business trips difficult to cope with, they might create a transitional routine. For example, each evening before a trip, they eat Chinese food and watch a movie. In the morning, they kiss good-bye and say, "See ya later, alligator." When he returns from a trip, he brings pizza, and they spend the evening talking about the separate experiences they had while they were apart. These bookend rituals help Pamela feel grounded because they provide a comforting sense of routine in the midst of change.

A helper or aide who works with an ASD individual can teach him what to expect in his routine daily schedule, but also to count on at least one unexpected event happening during the day. Part of his end-of-day routine might involve talking about the unexpected events that occurred on that particular day. The aide is essentially teaching him that the unexpected *is* expected. This does not remove the stress entirely, but it does allow the unexpected to have a place within the day, even if that place is unknown when the day begins.

Individuals with ASD often prefer to know what will happen next. They often do not care for surprises, even if they are good ones. These might be the people who read the end of the book first, or who prefer to know what they are getting for Christmas rather than having a big surprise on Christmas morning. Allowing ASD individuals to have this bit of predictability can make the day-to-day uncertainties of life easier to handle.

Patient Scenario: Timothy

Timothy was a seventy-two-year-old widower. Every morning he walked five blocks to morning Mass and then walked home. He had two pieces of toast and two cups of black coffee for breakfast. He then walked the dog and came back to read the newspaper. For lunch, he ate two hot dogs and had another two cups of black coffee. After watching the news and weather in the afternoon, he ate toast with raspberry jam. The next day, he started the routine again.

His daughter went with him to speak with his primary care physician about his repetitive and restricted eating routine. Because the physician understood Timothy's diagnosis of ASD, he tried to work with Timothy and his daughter to improve some aspects of his nutrition.

They ended up with a somewhat different routine including some vitamins, a chocolate Ensure drink with fiber in the evening, and a 32-ounce container of water that he tried to finish by the end of the day. The additional vitamins, fiber, and fluids did seem to improve his health somewhat, but Timothy remained very resistant to any further changes in his diet.

Emotional Self-Control

Emotional self-control refers to the ability to manage one's emotions. When an individual experiences emotion, his brain is in charge of interpreting and labeling the emotion. It is also in charge of regulating the intensity of the emotion, deciding how to handle the emotion, and communicating with others while in the midst of the emotion. Individuals in the autism spectrum often have difficulties with emotional self-control. These difficulties usually take one of three forms: shutting down, explosive behavior, or anxiety and rigidity.

Patient Scenario: Edward

Edward did not sleep well the night before he accompanied his wife to an afternoon wedding for her coworker. The wedding reception was crowded, and he met many people he did not know. There was small talk and dancing. When they returned home, he went to his study and sat in his favorite chair. His wife attempted to engage him in conversation about the day, but he seemed to ignore her, at times even avoid her. She didn't understand why he had been so shut off to himself at the reception, and she was irritated that he hadn't been more supportive of her attempts to impress her boss. (She was hoping for a promotion at work.) His wife didn't understand that Edward felt tired and overwhelmed from being in a crowd of people. His retreat to solitude was his response to difficulties with emotional self-control.

Patient Scenario: Becca

Becca typically went to her grandmother's house while her mother was at work. She always took a backpack with a book and her lunch, which always consisted of a peanut butter and jelly sandwich, Pringles, and an apple juice. On Wednesday, she was packed and ready to go as usual when her mother received a call that her grandmother had fallen and been taken to the hospital. Becca and her mother needed to quickly change plans and go to the emergency room at the local hospital. They left in a hurry and weren't sure what they would find when they arrived, nor did they know when they would return home. Becca found the hospital chaotic and uncertain. The strong smells irritated her, and the many strangers who came in and out of the room made her feel nervous and disjointed.

Grandmother didn't look like herself, and that upset Becca most of all. To cope with her feelings, she went to the corner of the room, sat on the floor, wrapped her arms around her legs, and rocked herself back and forth. She asked to go home so she could eat her lunch at a table, but Mother said they couldn't leave. Becca said she couldn't eat lunch without a table. Before anyone knew what was happening, Becca was yelling and crying that she needed to leave, she needed a table, she needed to eat. Becca's strong reaction to the unexpected change in her schedule, her routine, and her daily environment reflected her difficulties with emotional regulation and balance.

Patient Scenario: Jake

Jake was driving home from a particularly busy and stressful day at his job as a cashier. It was the holiday season, which meant the store was more crowded and fast-paced than usual. Some of his customers were kind and wished him a Merry Christmas, while others were critical and irritable. To make things worse, on his normal route home, traffic was diverted toward a detour because of a water main break.

By the time he reached home, he was on edge and anxious. His wife had rearranged the living room furniture where he was planning to watch the football game on TV. His favorite easy chair was still there, but it was at a different angle, which changed his view of the screen. Rather than being able to sit and eat dinner first to ease into the evening, he put down his things and moved the furniture back the way it was. He felt anxious, rigid, and unable to cope with the way his evening was unfolding. He was unable to explain what was bothering him. His wife mistakenly thought he was giving her the silent treatment. Actually, he was having problems managing the emotions that swept over him at the end of this very long and difficult day. He wasn't trying to punish her or get out of explaining; he was just trying to arrange his life so that he could calm down.

Difficulties regulating emotion and responding in a balanced manner are common in the autism spectrum. Chapter 10 will outline strategies to help ASD individuals with emotional resilience and regulation.

Before we move on, let's talk about Mr. Allen from the beginning of our chapter. Remember how his wife brought him in so that his "depression" could be fixed? She had created an explanation for herself that gave meaning to their situation. She decided that he was grieving his retirement, even though Mr. Allen had not expressed any particular emotional or internal struggle. Once we discussed his developmental history and the scope of his adult life, it became apparent that he met criteria for autism spectrum. Not every part of his history is relevant to this chapter, but let me highlight the difficulty that retirement presented for him.

Mr. Allen was under-responsive to his environment. He didn't notice a lot that was going on around him. He was, perhaps, similar to the absent-minded professor portrayed in stories, but he could follow directions from others, and generally tried to be compliant with the rules. He did not, however, have an internal direction or drive without external structure. His work had been predictable. He had a set work schedule, one office, and similar projects throughout his career. He even traveled at times, although someone else arranged his itinerary, bought his airline tickets, drove him to the airport, and picked him up. He was a good follower. Without the predictable external structure of his job, he was a bit lost—not depressed, just without direction. He had always been without internal drive and direction, but his environment had provided that for him. He needed more structure at home, and his wife needed a context in which to understand his behavior.

Executive function was the missing piece.

Chapter 5

A Sensational World

The world communicates to us all the time. It is filled with the buzzing of insects, the soft whisper of the wind on our skin, and the sweet scent of flowers in the air. It is filled with the blaring of horns in the busy streets and the smells of sweat and garbage in the alleys. Whether at a carnival or a cathedral, sensations fill the air, and our senses are bombarded with information about our world.

Eight Senses

Although we are generally taught about five senses, many would argue we actually have eight senses. :

1. **Taste**: Our taste buds can detect sweet, bitter, sour, salty and umami (a pleasant savory taste found in meat, fish, vegetables, and dairy products)

2. **Smell**: Our nose has hundreds of olfactory receptors that detect scent. Smell and taste combine to create our sense of food flavors.

3. **Hearing**: The ears perceive sound when they take in vibrations carried through the air and into the various sections of the ear.

4. **Sight**: Our eyes take in visible light, which is translated through nerve impulses into information about colors, hues, and brightness.

5. **Touch**: The somatosensory system in the skin detects texture, temperature, pressure, and pain.

6. **Movement**: The vestibular sense has its seat in the inner ear canals and helps us know where our bodies are in space. It detects information about our body's relationship to gravity (G-force), movement (acceleration and deceleration), and balance (body movements and the position of the head).

7. **Proprioception**: This is the sense of where our limbs and body parts are in relationship to each other. For example, even when our eyes are closed, we are aware of our arms and whether they are still or moving. This body sense helps us plan and coordinate movements such as hitting a baseball or flipping off the diving board without having to see where we are in space or thinking through each part of the movement to complete it.

8. **Interoception**: This sense relays information to the brain about what is happening inside our bodies, such as internal pain, temperature, heartbeat, hunger, thirst, breathing, and bowel/bladder elimination. It is separate from information from the skin (mechanoreception) or from the muscles and joints (proprioception). This information helps us know if we are hungry or sick, for example.

Although we have sensory organs that take in information from our world, these sensations must be processed through the brain and given meaning. Our brain is what tells us if the sensation is strong or subtle, continuous or sporadic, painful or comforting, new or old, and dangerous or safe.

Our brain also filters the information. When the filtering function in the brain works optimally, it mutes unimportant information while highlighting meaningful and essential information.

For example, during a work lecture, you can typically filter out the sound of your colleague breathing, the texture of your shirt collar, the pressure of the chair, and the smell of the cleaning fluid used to sanitize the room. Your brain lets go of those sensations while focusing on the tone and volume of the speaker's voice, the emotions and facial expressions of the speaker, and the information presented.

For individuals with brain connections that do not process sensations efficiently or in a way that is appropriate to the setting or environment, the brain may communicate all sorts of extraneous sensory information while the individual is trying to focus on the lecture. The listener may be receiving signals that his body needs more movement and pressure, thus making it hard for him to sit still.

His brain may be unable to release the sound of the fluorescent lights buzzing, making it hard to focus on the topic of the meeting. Likewise, he may be unable to correctly process the speaker's facial expressions and prosody (emotions of the voice), which causes him to misunderstand the importance of what has been relayed in the meeting.

Sensory Processing Dysfunction

Impaired sensory processing is a common symptom in developmental conditions, although it can occur after brain injury as well. Developmental sensory processing difficulties can occur alone or in combination with other conditions such as attention deficit disorder. An over-reactivity or under-reactivity to sensory inputs is one of the criteria that can be used in diagnosing autism, as stated in the DSM-5:

> Hyper- or hypo-reactivity to sensory input or unusual interests in sensory aspects of the environment (for example, apparent indifference to pain/temperature, adverse response to specific sounds or textures, excessive smelling or touching of objects, visual fascination with lights or movement)

It has been estimated that 42 to 88 percent of individuals in the spectrum have a history of sensory processing difficulties. Some patients and families I work with report that sensory processing difficulties were more prominent during childhood than adulthood, although impaired sensory processing in adulthood is also common.

Sensory processing dysfunction can look different across individuals and across the eight senses. One person may have quite a bit of trouble tolerating textures of clothing but love how certain body movements feel such as spinning, rocking, and swinging.

Another person may have very little tolerance for movement, and seem almost oblivious to the temperature, texture, and taste of foods, eating anything set before them.

An ASD individual may be generally under-reactive to touch, not noticing when her hands or face are dirty or when she steps on something in her bare feet. She may also crave deep pressure but avoid movement. For instance, she may like to squeeze pillows on her lap, lay on her stomach when using the computer, or sleep under a pile of heavy blankets but complain of feeling dizzy on the stairs or getting carsick easily.

Individuals with sensory processing dysfunction may be labeled as inattentive, picky, or hyperactive, depending on what types of sensory inputs they are seeking, avoiding, or not noticing.

Changes from day to day can occur as well. Similar to how we all have good days and bad days, so too does the individual in the autism spectrum. One of my patients noted, "I know what kind of day I'm going to have by how it feels to brush my teeth." This particular gentleman knew that his body was struggling that day if he experienced significant touch aversion in his mouth when brushing his teeth in the morning. This signal from his body alerted him that he might have trouble tolerating basic activities more than usual that day.

Difficulties processing sensory information in a balanced and meaningful way can add to the anxiety that individuals in the spectrum often feel. Individuals with high sensitivities may display more rigid behaviors as they endeavor to keep their environment "just so" in an effort to decrease the amount of information they must process or adjust to. Unexpected events may feel like an onslaught of new information, whereas routine events and repetitive behaviors feel comforting and predictable.

In contrast, those who are typically under-reactive can appear passive in their environment and nonresponsive to others. They may seem to be in their own little world. Others may view them as lazy or uninterested because they do not respond to what needs to be done at home (oblivious to stacks of dirty dishes), or practice basic hygiene (taking a shower, brushing teeth, using deodorant), or reliably acknowledge when someone else is in the room, a trait that can be particularly challenging when receiving visitors.

Sensory Inputs

In addition to using sensory inputs to make sense of the world around us, we also use sensory information to self-regulate. Just as a car needs the ability to speed up or slow down based on the circumstances, we need the ability to wake up and become attentive and alert, along with the ability to calm down and relax. A balanced and centered internal state is vital for productivity and comfort. It is important to become alert in the morning and to wind down at night. We need the ability to stay calm during intense emotional moments. We need the ability to feel the urgency to complete important tasks. The capacity to tone down or turn up our alertness and engagement with our surroundings is called self-regulation.

All of us use sensation to achieve this regulation. In the morning, we may need a hot shower, a scented lotion, and an aromatic cup of coffee to become awake and alert for our morning tasks, which prepares us for interacting with others.

After an intense meeting at work, we may use the movement of pacing in our office to release some pent-up tension. Some of us may chew gum or squeeze a stress ball during the day to stay alert or stay calm.

After a stressful day at work, we may come home to the chaos of kids arguing and wish we could lock ourselves in the bathroom to get some quiet time. Alternatively, we may regulate ourselves by going out for a brisk run. After the kids are in bed, a soak in the tub and a scented candle may help us regulate down to a state of restfulness and sleep.

Although many of us also use our thoughts *(The kids are just as tired and hungry as I am. I need to calm down)*, self-regulation is not achieved with thoughts alone, but also through sensations. The individual with sensory processing difficulties has challenges with self-regulation. The amount of sensory input he needs to stay alert and calm may be significantly different from the general population. One person in the autism spectrum may need to swing at the local park for thirty minutes before he can feel calm. Another may need the lights down and sound-cancelling headphones to feel centered. Yet another may need to jump on a trampoline or jump rope before work in order to "turn on" his attention.

We also use sensory experiences to help us regulate our emotional responses. Individuals in the spectrum are often under or over-reactive to emotions as well as physical sensations. Some would argue that there is so much physical experience to emotions that perhaps this difficulty is one core problem with processing internal input. There are likely to be emotional cues in the environment that autistics miss, but it is also true that many individuals in the spectrum are hyper-reactive to emotional content. Because it is difficult for these individuals to cope with emotional situations, they may show dysregulation in the midst of emotion by shutting down, seeking sensory inputs, and/or having emotional meltdowns.

An over-reactivity to emotions and sensations is described in the Intense World Theory of autism. This theory suggests that glutamate, the major excitatory neurotransmitter in the brain, may be over-functioning in the circuits of the neocortex of the ASD individual's brain, leading to hypersensitivity to the environment. The theory discusses four areas of over-functioning, including hyper-perception (taking in too much sensory information), hyper-attention (fixation of attention on small details), hyper-memory (significant memory for small details), and hyper-emotionality (difficulty regulating emotional experience and expression). Researchers suggest that the pattern of sensitivities in these four areas may account for some of the over-reactivity in certain individuals with autism.

Just as all of us use sensory inputs to regulate alertness and calm, individuals in the spectrum also frequently benefit from strategically using certain inputs to bring about a more centered state. These inputs should be part of a daily routine to improve internal balance. The individual can also use certain inputs as needed when he feels unusually overwhelmed or sluggish and needs to return to a more centered state.

Sensory inputs to help with self-regulation may include some combination of deep pressure, joint sensation, and movement.

Deep Pressure and Joint Input

Although individuals in the spectrum can have a variety of challenges with sensory inputs, it is generally true that deep pressure and joint input can produce a calming and alerting response. For the individual who is under-responsive to the environment and seems "cloudy" or "spacy," this type of input can feel alerting and focusing. For the individual who is over-responsive to the environment and seems anxious or hypersensitive, this type of input can feel calming and centering. The engagement in deep pressure and joint input can be part of an overall lifestyle program to cope with sensory issues.

Deep pressure input is anything that puts pressure on the body. It can involve a variety of things such as bear hugs, massage, or resting in a snug hammock. It may involve lying on one's stomach to work on a project rather than sitting in a chair. Some individuals obtain deep pressure input through swimming (water pressure) or using weighted blankets, weighted vests, or pressure vests. There are even vests and jackets on the market now that can be inflated to provide a comforting pressure while maintaining the look of a regular jacket. The amount of air pressure can be adjusted from day to day to meet the changing needs of the individual.

Lifting, pushing, or pulling actions provide joint input. Three systems can be the focus of joint input: whole body, mouth and jaw, and hands.

- **Whole body activities:** In whole body activities, multiple joints are moving and receiving input at one time or in sequence. Activities can be chosen that have a daily function (carrying heavy items), are pleasurable (riding a bicycle), or involve an exercise routine (stretching a Thera-Band). Specific activities may include carrying groceries, carrying a heavy backpack, stacking chairs, pulling on a rope, shoveling snow, swimming, jumping on a trampoline, crab walking, washing windows, sanding a wood-working project, doing yoga poses, digging with a shovel, or pulling weeds.

- **Mouth and jaw:** Activities that involve the mouth and jaw may include chewing, sucking, or blowing. Specific activities may consist of chewing gum, beef jerky, taffy or other resistive foods; sucking a thick smoothie through a thin straw or using the tongue to work through a spoonful of peanut butter against the roof of the mouth; blowing through a straw, blowing up balloons, or blowing through a whistle or musical instrument.

- **Hands:** Activities with the hands may include kneading bread, brushing a dog, squeezing a stress ball, making something out of clay or Theraputty, playing with silly putty, using a spray bottle, or squeezing the sprayer on a hose.

The Use of Movement

In addition to using deep pressure and joint input to help the body feel alert and calm, other sensory experiences can also provide important input. Some individuals seek movement in order to feel centered and alert, while others avoid movement, complain of feeling dizzy, and always like to have their feet on the floor.

For those who seek movement, there is often a difference between linear and rotary movement.

- **Linear vestibular input:** This results when an individual is moving in a straight line (forward and back or left to right). This type of movement can be calming and centering, particularly if not too vigorous or with quickly changing directions. We can all relate to how calming a gentle rocking movement is to a stressed baby. Babies often fall asleep in a moving car, feeling calmed by the gentle linear movement. Adults experience linear movement when using a rocking chair, swinging on a porch swing, or even moving back and forth to a song or while talking to others. In contrast to gentle linear movement, vigorous linear movement can be quite alerting. It can be obtained by jumping on a trampoline, riding a motorcycle, or running.

- **Rotary vestibular input:** Rotary movement involves moving in a circle rather than a line. Circular movements are generally alerting rather than calming, although this may differ between individuals. An individual may benefit from alerting input if he is having trouble staying awake, paying attention, or maintaining focus while learning new information. Circular movements can be obtained by riding on spinning rides at a park or a carnival, spinning around in rotating chairs, or rolling one's body down a hill.

- **Inversion movements:** Inversion occurs anytime the head moves below the heart. This type of movement can also be centering and may involve things like hanging upside down on a jungle gym bar or performing the down-dog position in yoga.

Strategies to Reduce Sensory Overload

In addition to using certain sensory inputs for calming and alerting, the ASD individual may also want to use certain strategies to reduce sensory overload and drain. Because the typical daily environment may feel intense to the autistic individual, balancing how much input to process throughout the day and using additional inputs for calming and alerting is a good way to improve self-regulation.

- **Assistive devices:** One way to manage the amount of sensory input the person has to process is to use assistive devices. An assistive device is anything that helps someone perform a task that most individuals can perform without a device. ASD individuals may use assistive devices in their daily life to decrease adverse sensory inputs. For example, gloves can be used when gardening or washing dishes. Some individuals may like to use sunglasses or baseball caps to block out extra visual inputs. Others who are sensitive to sound may prefer to wear earplugs or sound-cancelling headphones or to use white noise machines in their work or personal environments. Those who are sensitive to smells may wish to put a dab of scented lotion or perfume on the skin under their noses, or even wear a mask while doing smelly tasks such as handling the garbage or cleaning the bathroom.

- **Changing the environment:** Individuals with sensory integration difficulty may also focus on changing their environments to better suit their needs. One person may close the shades in the house during the day, while another may keep the TV on a low volume. It is common for sensory sensitive individuals to only wear clothing made of fabrics that are not itchy and do not irritate their skin, and to make sure the tags are cut out.

They may limit their food choices based on smell, taste, or texture. Likewise, purchases of personal items such as toothpaste, shampoo, and lotions may also be based largely on the very specific textures and scents the individual prefers because she craves those scents or textures. For instance, she may seek vanilla scents but hate peppermint. Vanilla shampoo fills her senses with pleasant sensations, thus making her want to shower more frequently. Avoiding peppermint toothpaste and using a different flavor helps her brush her teeth regularly.

- **Recuperation strategies:** Individuals in the autism spectrum often need recuperation strategies after being out in the community, as the overall exposure to sensations and unexpected events can be mentally, emotionally, and physically draining. Recuperation strategies may include the calming and alerting sensory experiences we discussed earlier (joint input, deep pressure, vestibular input), but can also include time in an environment with low sensory inputs such as reading while reclining underneath a cover, quiet time alone, and spending time doing familiar, preferable activities such as retreating to watch favorite movies or YouTube videos.

In addition to self-regulation strategies, the individual may want to seek the input and recommendations of an Occupational Therapist (OT) who specializes in ASD. Among other things, the OT therapist specializes in identifying and suggesting interventions for sensory regulation difficulties. Although many OT therapists work exclusively with children in the spectrum, some are branching into serving the needs of the adult and geriatric populations as well. A skilled therapist can identify areas of over- and under-reactivity to develop appropriate interventions and strategies unique to the individual.

Patient Scenario: Jeremy

Jeremy was a thirty-two-year-old young man who lived with his parents. He had completed special education programs while attending high school, but had only been given an autism diagnosis a year before he became my patient. After assessment, it was clear that many areas of functioning would benefit from intervention. In addition to social skills training and a job coach, one of the first goals was to better identify and treat his severe sensory processing symptoms. These symptoms were largely responsible for his seclusion at home, which in turn reduced his engagement with his medical team and therapy staff, and decreased his overall independent functioning and ability to work with a job coach.

After an occupational therapy assessment was conducted by a skilled therapist in his home environment, it was clear that Jeremy had several areas of sensory over-reactivity and under-reactivity. He seemed over-reactive to light and noise, but he was under-reactive to touch and smell. His over-reactivity led him to stay in the house with the blinds drawn and the TV off, and his under-reactivity made it difficult for him to know when he needed to brush his teeth or take a shower.

Among other home interventions, his therapist worked to set up a "sensory diet" for him. A sensory diet is a list of certain sensory activities he performs daily to help regulate his alertness, attention, and sense of calm. In addition, she suggested he use assistive devices—sunglasses, noise cancelling headphones, and a weighted baseball cap—to decrease some of the inputs that assaulted his senses whenever he went outside. A list of sensory strategies that could be used when he felt unexpectedly overwhelmed was also developed. These first steps were part of a larger intervention strategy for helping this gentleman live a fuller life. By improving his sensory integration, his ability to function comfortably from day to day flourished.

Chapter 6

Relationships

A myth about individuals in the autism spectrum is that they have no close relationships and no desire for relationships. Believers of this myth may rule out a diagnosis of ASD on the basis of the individual having some type of close relationship. In truth, it is difficult to find a solid statistic regarding the percentage of individuals in the autism spectrum who maintain long-term relationships, and what those relationships look like.

This difficulty is due to a number of reasons, primarily the under-diagnosing of adults, particularly those in older age groups, but also because the diagnostic criteria have changed over the years. Furthermore, older studies often excluded those with diagnoses such as Asperger's syndrome and Pervasive Developmental Disorder, individuals who would likely have a diagnosis of ASD in the current classification system.

Research demonstrates that individuals with autism tend to be in fewer long-term peer relationships than the general population. For example, Farley et al. (2009) studied forty-one individuals who had been diagnosed with classic autism in childhood twenty years earlier (not including Asperger's disorder or Pervasive Developmental Disorder-NOS). Each of the study participants was documented as having low average intellectual functioning, which means their IQs primarily were in the 80s. Statistics regarding the frequency of long-term relationships included the finding that 44 percent of the participants had never dated, and only 19 percent were or had been in long-term relationships at the time of the study. It was noted that 85 percent regularly attended church activities, representing a kind of structured, group interaction that provided a comfortable form of social interaction.

Similarly, in a study looking only at the "classic autism" population, Orsmond et al. (2004) examined the social functioning of 235 adolescents and young adults aged ten to twenty-one years. These individuals were rated across four levels of peer relationships:

- Same-aged friend with whom s/he enjoyed varied, mutually responsive, and reciprocal activities outside of an organized setting. Just over 8 percent had at least one friendship like this.

- Relationship involving some activities outside of a prearranged setting: 20.9 percent

- Relationships only in prearranged settings: 24.3 percent

- No peer relationships: 46.4 percent

This study was interesting in that it examined not only the presence of relationships but also the degree of age-appropriate relationships. Having same-aged friends and enjoying mutually responsive and varied interactions is commonly found in neurotypical adult populations. These relationships are reciprocal in that they involve a back-and-forth of ideas and activities, some of which occur outside a structured setting with prearranged activities.

Individuals in the autistic spectrum were more likely to describe individuals they were "friendly with" in a structured setting such as a church youth group or a chess club. They often indicated that they were closest with their family members and had no clear reciprocal relationships outside of immediate family.

Many of the adult autistics I work with describe having friendships. It is only when asked what they do with their friends and how often they spend time with them that it becomes apparent there is a lack of true connection. For example, an ASD individual may name two friends that they have relationships with, only to state that they attended high school together (a structured setting), and over the last thirty years have talked to each other on the phone about twice a year. Another individual may relate that he has many online gaming friends and proceed to list their online names and note that they have never connected in person or done any activity together other than gaming. It is not that this is not a valid form of connection with others, but rather that the connections do not have the same frequency and quality as neurotypical age-appropriate relationships built on shared in-person experiences. It is also true that after an ASD individual graduates or retires, the lack of a structured setting in which to make relationships significantly hinders his or her connection with others.

Additionally, many of the young adults I work with have an acute sense of grief that they are not connected to others the same way their peers are. Particularly during young adulthood when students graduate high school and go off to university, build their careers, and start families, ASD individuals describe a deep longing for achieving these same milestones. They often describe the difficulties they experience reaching these goals.

Alternatively, they may long for age appropriate connections as a way to be the same as others, but struggle with actually managing relationships when they do find love and true friendship. For example, the ASD individual may have longed for marriage and children, only to feel overwhelmed by the closeness of others in his personal environment when he becomes a husband and father. It may be that the dream is more attractive than the reality in these cases.

The current diagnostic criteria for ASD depict a wider range of cognitive and communicative abilities than the previous diagnosis for autism. Therefore, studies using the new diagnostic criteria most likely capture a wider range of relationship connections in the spectrum. However, it is also likely that individuals in the spectrum have fewer mature, reciprocal peer relationships outside of prearranged settings than the general population. There are likely many factors that contribute to this tendency.

Struggles with Social Communication

The difficulties that ASD individuals have with social communication can negatively impact their ability to connect with others. They are more likely to struggle with reading between the lines, understanding humor, and being able to identify and express emotional content.

Most would agree that the hardest part of a marriage or long-term peer relationship is the issue of communication. Even the best communicators wrestle with the issues of "I didn't mean that" and "You should know when I need more help." When someone within the autism spectrum is in a close relationship with another person, both individuals in that relationship benefit from having a specific understanding of the common communication pitfalls in the spectrum. Expectations for communication need to be adjusted within the framework of ASD and what the autistic individual is capable of doing or learning to do. Relationship counseling or psychotherapy should generally be more focused on concrete issues of communication strategies and social skills training rather than emphasizing techniques involving insight, metaphor, and analogy.

Difficulty Regulating Emotions

Within the autism spectrum, there are differences in how the individual experiences, processes, and communicates emotion. Certainly, some autistic individuals tend to be data- and thought-oriented without much range of emotion. For example, one gentleman told me his greatest fear is that when his parents die, he "won't feel anything." When I asked another young woman what she thinks her life will be like after her parents pass away, she stated, "No different, really. I can still be in the same house."

Others, however, feel the same range of strong emotions as neurotypical individuals, but have difficulties in the following areas:

- Describing emotions
- Identifying the degree of emotion such as recognizing the signs of a large buildup of overwhelming emotion
- Managing the emotions of others, specifically by separating themselves from the distress of another individual
- Regulating their own emotional experience so that they can feel emotions while also calming themselves

These individuals may avoid emotional content (conflict with others, grief and loss, declarations of endearment) because it feels overwhelming. These difficulties in managing emotional content can challenge the health and longevity of relationships. It is important for neurotypical individuals who are in emotional relationships with ASD individuals not to attribute a shutting down during emotional conversation as a disregard for the well-being of others.

Questions that sound like accusations will only push the ASD individual away, such as "Why do you always leave the room when we talk about something important? Don't you care enough about me to work on improving our relationship?"

One strategy that neurotypical individuals can use to navigate emotional communications with autistic individuals is to build in some distance when it comes to emotional content and conversation. For example, she may talk best about emotions after some time has passed after the initial event. If there has been a difficult interaction, allowing time and space for her to process what happened and to return to a more centered state may improve the overall quality of the conversation later. Another way to create helpful distance is to allow various forms of communication other than face-to-face talks. She may prefer to leave her partner a letter or send an email about her thoughts and feelings so she doesn't have to process her partner's facial expressions and emotions while talking. This gives the ASD individual better resilience and problem-solving skills when the couple decides to talk about their relationships, conflicts, and emotions.

The Need for Alone Time

Many people in the autism spectrum seek alone time. Although they may enjoy certain social contacts, the interactions with others are less likely to fill them up than alone time. This type of tendency can certainly work in relationships, but there may be a need for the partner to seek some degree of alone time as well. In the long term, an extrovert may not receive the amount of interaction she needs from an autistic partner, most of whom are more introverted.

Some individuals have remarked that their ASD partner was so interactive before they had children or before he got a full-time job, for example. This can be the case if the ASD individual needs a certain amount of down time to refuel, and the children or his job take up time that he previously spent with his partner. Too many activities and too much multi-tasking is difficult for the ASD individual, whereas more extroverted individuals feel energized by meeting new people and participating in activities with others.

For the ASD individual, comfortable routines feel good, whereas many neurotypical individuals seek novelty and excitement, unexpected events, and surprises. Having a friend or partner with compatible needs is important for the long-term health of the relationship.

"Parallel Play" in Adulthood

Another thing that can be present in adult ASD relationships with some frequency is a type of "parallel play." Parallel play is a developmental stage of interaction usually seen around two to three years of age. It is called parallel play because the two children are busy playing next to each other with separate activities, but they aren't playing with each other. For example, one plays with trucks while the other one paints. Each child shows interest in what the other is doing but does not try to significantly change or alter the other person's play or involve that child in his or her play.

As children get older, their play tends to be more reciprocal and interactive. Everyone continues to have some parallel play into older ages, but the ASD individual may continue with more than most.

In adulthood, parallel activities may include reading in the same room while your partner works a crossword puzzle. The ASD individual considers this type of parallel activity as spending time together, whereas the non-ASD partner feels lonely and left out because there is no true, face-to-face interaction. Each partner has a different need for parallel versus interactive social contact.

Dependence on Others

Although many ASD individuals seek less interaction with people than the general population, they often do not prefer to be completely on their own or independent. Often, the individual actually seems somewhat dependent on others for guidance, support, and structure. They may seem to feel lost in their own world without supportive, external guidance.

It is in this context that they may actually have an incorrect diagnosis of dependent personality disorder. An example of this would be a young woman who hasn't moved out of her parents' home and is unable to make independent decisions.

Some autistics gravitate toward relationships that provide support and caring, but also some degree of alone time and a lower level of emotional demand. They may prefer to interact with others in the context of a prearranged structured activity, such as school or work, church activities, political club, nature group, or an activity with a built-in routine, such as always watching *Star Wars* when a certain person comes to visit. They may be closest with a family member or friend who helps them with daily activities and decisions.

Some autistics avoid conflict because of their fear of being alone. They don't want to anger their support person(s) because they're afraid that will make them not want to be with them anymore. Although they don't like crowds, and they don't seek out contact with people, most do not want to be completely alone because they find it hard to navigate the world. Their "close" people help them feel safe. Some ASD individuals may feel that their "close person" is a lifeline in daily activities.

Rigid Thought Patterns and Difficulty Understanding the Views of Others

In contrast to the avoidance of conflict shown by some autistic individuals, others seem to be magnets for conflict. These individuals tend to have strong and rigid views, and show an inability to see more than one side of an issue. They seem unable to take in and consider information that is new or that differs from their own experiences, thoughts, and ideas. They often seem argumentative, and others may describe them as narcissistic. They tend to bully others to believe or behave as they do.

This type of thought process can be quite difficult on relationships, and these individuals often drive others away. They are often considered difficult to work with and "poor team players." If they are good at their jobs, they may remain in positions of influence and authority where their forcefulness is seen as leadership. If they are poor workers, they often have a long history of failed jobs. It can be quite difficult for family members, counselors, and the medical team to positively impact these individuals' daily lives, and they often have a long history of "firing" professionals who try to help them.

Difficulty with Touch and Sensory Inputs

Many close adult relationships involve some amount of physical contact, something that may be difficult for the ASD adult to regulate in the presence of sensory processing difficulties. In general, light touch is often more aversive to individuals in the spectrum than deep pressure. Instead of lightly touching someone who is sensitive to touch, a bear hug may actually feel better. Some individuals with touch aversion have described light touch as painful or aversive, similar to feeling a bug crawling on your arm. But there is quite a bit of individual difference as to whether those in the spectrum avoid touch.

Also, individuals with sensory dysfunction often have fluctuations in how much they avoid certain sensations. They may avoid touch if they are "having a bad day" but seek physical contact if they are having a better day. Many individuals with autistic characteristics lack appropriate physical boundaries. They may, for example, sit too close to someone on the couch while watching a movie. They may need input as to how much physical closeness others want or need at any given time. An ASD individual and his partner can talk about what kinds of physical connections feel good and at what times.

Patient Scenario: Jacob and Jessica

Jacob and Jessica met online seven years ago, in person five years ago, and had their first of two children four years ago. They lived in an apartment, and Jacob worked as a machinist at a local shop. Jessica stayed at home with their two children. Jessica described Jacob as focused and attentive to her during the initial years of their relationship, but she was increasingly dissatisfied with their relationship. She was starved for interaction by the time Jacob came home from work, but he typically shut down and remained silent as a way to decompress from the workday. He did not interact with her and did not contribute to the household chores that needed to be done. He never spent time in the family room with Jessica and the children, but rather spent time in the bedroom on the computer with earphones on. Jessica wondered why he changed, and she felt like she was drowning in the responsibilities of running their household, raising their children, and keeping their family together.

They began attending marriage counseling, at which time Jacob was diagnosed with autism spectrum disorder. When this happened, a "light went on" for them both, as this diagnosis "explained so much." Because the counselor was experienced in working with individuals in the autism spectrum, his first goal was to educate them about their individual needs and ways of interacting. This added to their self-awareness and provided an explanation and context for what was happening between them. The counselor's second objective was to help them learn to communicate in ways that would improve their relationship.

One strategy involved using the magnetic numbers on the refrigerator that their kids played with. When Jacob returned to the apartment, he chose a number from 1 to 5 to express how he felt that day, with 1 being great and 5 being completely overwhelmed. He put it on the fridge next to Jessica's number for the day. This way, they could each have a visual idea of how their partner was feeling without needing a face-to-face discussion about it right when Jacob walked in the door. They gradually learned that they both were at a breaking point by that time of day.

Jacob still went into the bedroom and got on the computer, shutting out the world with earphones. After thirty minutes of alone time, he and Jessica texted each other from their separate rooms. This gave them the opportunity to connect, but also to be separate for a bit more time.

This tradition became a true bonding experience for them, as Jacob was able to joke and flirt with Jessica without having the kids crawling on him and without having too much interaction with Jessica when he first walked in the door feeling overwhelmed from work.

After about an hour, Jacob fed the kids dinner while Jessica went to her exercise class. When Jessica got home, she put the kids to bed while Jacob had more down time. They started a routine of watching their favorite TV series before Jessica went to bed. Jacob was a night owl, so he focused on some chores after Jessica went to bed. He hated dealing with the garbage or dishes because of the strong smells, but he liked doing the laundry and didn't mind putting the toys in bins in the living room before going to bed.

Their counselor was able to help them see that good family time often occurred outdoors where they could all have open space rather than the chaos of noise and touch that indoor apartment play could have on their family of four. Their relationship took a lot of work and creativity, but with their counselor's help, they found ways to create "space" and "closeness" in their marriage and family.

Chapter 7

Education, Employment, and Independent Living Skills

W e have discussed many diagnostic symptoms and associated features of the autism spectrum. This chapter will focus on education followed by the transition to adulthood and independent living.

The season of childhood and adolescence is generally spent within the context of the school system. As we noted earlier, some individuals in the spectrum are diagnosed while in school, and others are not. Within the public school setting, relatively recent changes have directly impacted the education of those with disabilities. Two federal laws enacted in 1975 set the ball rolling for recognition of and support for disabilities within the public school system: The Education for All Handicapped Children Act (EHA) and the Individuals with Disabilities Education Act (IDEA). The EHA establishes a right to public education for all children regardless of disability, while the IDEA requires that public schools provide individualized or "special education" for students with qualifying disabilities. At the time of this writing, many of the adults and geriatrics within the autism spectrum were educated prior to the implementation of these changes in the public school system. They did not benefit from this mandated recognition of disabilities and individualized education, and this lack of attention to their needs has followed them their entire lives.

History of Special Education Services in Schools

Prior to the 1980s, the diagnosis of autism did not exist, and during this decade, the autistic children identified generally had severe symptoms including significant intellectual disability. The understanding that about half of ASD individuals have average or above average intellectual functioning is relatively recent. Additionally, the diagnostic criteria have changed over time, and some individuals that may not have met criteria in the past may meet the current diagnostic criteria.

In the current public school system, if a child struggles to learn the basic educational curriculum, the school can perform assessments to create an individualized educational program (IEP) to meet the child's needs. There are thirteen diagnoses that may qualify the student for an IEP. These may include interventions such as speech therapy and accommodations such as extra breaks. Having a disability, however, does not automatically qualify a child for an IEP. There must be a clear impact on her ability to learn the basic curriculum in a standard classroom setting.

If an individual with a disability does not qualify for an IEP, he may qualify for individualized accommodations in the learning environment within a 504 plan. This type of plan can provide accommodations for a student who has received a medical diagnosis. These can include extra time for taking tests or being allowed to take breaks during the day, but not interventions such as speech therapy or occupational therapy.

Even for the student who receives an IEP, the interventions provided by the school are geared toward helping the child learn the basic curriculum such as working on fine motor skills for writing and improving communication with teachers and peers. They are not geared toward an overall intervention of the disability itself. For example, the student with autism may not be provided with sensory integration treatments if his sensory symptoms do not impact his time in the classroom. Outsourced therapeutic services would provide aspects of intervention not provided by the school.

Because the recognition of disabilities in public schools is only mandated if the student is unable to successfully complete the basic curriculum, many students with adequate grades are unrecognized as having a diagnosis of autism spectrum disorder. As noted earlier, a large-scale study conducted in the United Kingdom found that many children with high-functioning autism remain undetected in schools, as many of them have learned to mask their symptoms in the classroom. For every three known cases of autism in the school system there were two unidentified cases. A second study in South Korea found that many of the children identified in the spectrum were in regular school programs without having been diagnosed and without receiving additional support.

Unfortunately, the ASD students who are able to make it through their academics may manifest their symptoms in other ways such as behavioral problems. It is not uncommon for students to make it through the school day then fall apart at home.

For this reason, even though the student passes academics, a correct diagnosis is necessary, and community interventions are vital to help the individual learn strategies for self-regulation and independence outside the school environment and into adulthood.

Autism Diagnosis in Schools

It is common for the individual with ASD to have more difficulties in certain environments and seasons of life than others. They typically have more difficulty in middle school and high school than they had in elementary school due to the increased demand for independence and executive function skills as well as the presence of more complex social environments.

Likewise, an individual with ASD may do relatively well in a school environment because of the amount of structure involved, but struggle greatly after graduation when he is required to schedule his own life. When he is in school, he knows what his class schedule is, he follows a book for his coursework, and he knows that eighth grade follows seventh grade.

However, after graduating high school, the individual is faced with a blank slate of possibility. For many in the spectrum, the vast open-ended options are difficult to maneuver. He has to decide whether to go to college, which college to attend, and what major to pursue. He is expected to independently manage multiple aspects of his education including applications, financial aid forms, and transportation to and around a campus. He will be expected to initiate interactions with other people such as his advisor, professors, and registrar staff. Organizational skills, conceptual learning, multi-tasking, planning, and prioritization are of significant importance. The student needs to initiate his own behaviors to do laundry, complete assignments, and eat regularly.

In response to this need, several universities are initiating autism support programs. Students at these schools who have been diagnosed with ASD qualify for support in the areas of social relationships and opportunities as well as in planning and prioritizing their studies. These students meet regularly with a mentor to help prevent the silent decline that some students experience when no one makes the student's success and well-being a priority. The mentor makes sure the student is on track with academics and facilitates ongoing communication among professors and advisors.

Transitioning from School to Independent Living and Employment

The transition from student to independent adult is often a period during which ASD individuals flounder, in part due to an abrupt decrease in the structure of their environment and a scarcity of resources to support the autistic at this life stage, particularly for those who do not have an intellectual disability.

Taylor et al. (2011) studied 66 young adults who had graduated from the secondary school system roughly two years prior. Three-fourths of the individuals were reported to have an intellectual disability. Fourteen percent of these individuals were taking classes toward a post-secondary degree, and most of these were also employed part time. Six percent of the young adults were competitively employed (they worked independently in jobs that required basic skills, such as busing tables, replacing dirty glasses with clean ones), earned enough money to pay their basic living expenses, and were not taking college courses. Of these, none were working full time.

An additional 12 percent worked in a supportive employment setting for individuals with disabilities, staffed with professionals to supervise their work. They earned some money but not enough to fully support their basic needs. This included jobs such as folding towels at a hotel and shredding documents. Fifty-six percent attended day programs, and nearly all of these had intellectual disability.

ASD individuals without an intellectual disability were three times more likely to be competitively employed than those with intellectual disability (ID). Additionally, 47 percent of those without ID were in post-secondary education programs compared to 2 percent of those with ID. Those without intellectual disability were far less likely to receive any type of adult day service (6 percent) than those with ID (74 percent).

The researchers noted that their findings were consistent with past research, which reported that under-employment is common within the ASD community.

There is a subgroup of young adults in the spectrum with functional intellect who seem to be at risk for under-employment specifically due to their repetitive and maladaptive behaviors. Taylor and Seltzer (2010) found that improvement in maladaptive behaviors in ASD slowed after leaving high school for those without ID as compared to those with ID. The possibly was raised by the researchers that the difference may reflect the relative lack of stimulating activities after secondary education and limited community supports and services for those who are in the autism spectrum but who do not have intellectual impairment. In other words, because of their intellectual ability, their needs are often overlooked.

Taylor et al. (2011) noted, "As hypothesized, a significant subgroup (nearly 25 percent) of the young adults in our sample who had ASD without ID were in this category, and those without ID were three times more likely to have no day activities than youths with ASD who also had comorbid ID. This divergent pattern likely does not represent a lack of abilities on the part of the youths with ASD, but instead the inadequacy of the current service system to accommodate the needs of youths with ASD who do not have ID as they are transitioning to adulthood. Indeed, only 18 percent of young adults without ID were getting some sort of employment or vocational services (e.g., supported employment, sheltered workshop) compared to 86 percent of young adults with ID."

The researchers emphasize the need for increased transitional services "that allow youths with ASD who do not have ID to achieve their maximum level of independence and develop sustainable careers. The current developmental disability service system does not appear to be accommodating the unique needs of individuals with ASD without ID." The researchers also encourage future research to see how successful the post-secondary education of ASD young adults may be in leading to work that is self-sustaining.

Impact of ASD on Independent Living Skills

Indeed, while enrolled in primary and secondary school, all students are provided with predictability and support, as well as a clear structure of options, but adulthood does not provide these. The individual with autism may want to move forward in life as his childhood peers are doing, but feels constrained or unable to do so because he has little to no structure and support to bring this goal to fruition.

Many ASD individuals leave high school and flounder because of the lack of clear direction. The relationships they had in the structured setting of school fade away, and the developmental tasks typical for their age group—full-time employment, independent living, marriage, parenthood—seem impossible to attain. They often have a strong sense of grief that they are not in the same stages of life as their peers, but they are unsure as to what goals are reasonable and achievable. The process of finding an appropriate job, managing long-term finances, paying immediate bills, and securing transportation can feel like a

Herculean task, not to mention navigating intimate relationships in pursuit of a life partner.

Farley et al. (2009) studied independent living in ASD individuals with average or low average intellect. Regarding living arrangements, they found that 7 percent lived in a home they purchased themselves, 5 percent lived independently in their own apartments, and 56 percent lived with their parents. Family members rating participants on the amount of daily assistance needed described 27 percent as needing a low level of help, 27 percent as needing a moderate level of help, and 46 percent as needing a high level of assistance.

Assistance for adults with ASD may be needed across several areas including housing, household cleaning, personal hygiene, purchasing needed items such as clothes and food, transportation, seeking and maintaining employment, healthcare and medications, financial management, and assisting with paperwork and agency requirements ranging from applications for community programs to paying taxes.

Housing

Housing options may come in different forms depending on the amount of supervision required for the person to live independently and the community in which she lives. As noted earlier, about 50 percent of adults in the autism spectrum live with family members who often provide some level of assistance. Farley et al. (2009) described 12 percent of adults with autism as living independently in a home or apartment. Living options with supervision in the community may include adult foster care, group homes, or supervised living programs for those with intellectual or developmental disabilities. All in all, the individual benefits from some form of assistance, although the amount and type of assistance varies from person to person.

Household Cleaning

The ability of the ASD individual to demonstrate appropriate cleanliness also varies quite a bit from one person to another. As with other ASD features, the individual may show too much attention to cleanliness and structure in some aspects of life and not enough in others. One individual may live sparsely, not buying new things and never replacing worn-out furniture in his living space.

Others may want to keep everything and live in a cluttered space, perhaps with piles of items in one place and collections of "special objects" such as maps or pencils in another. It is also common for executive function impairments to interfere with an ASD individual's success with home cleaning and maintenance. These impairments are evidenced by poor organization, difficulties initiating household tasks, and lack of attention to detail, which in this case means not noticing when the house is dirty or cluttered.

Sparse Living

The individual who lives sparsely may cite concerns about spending money to buy a new roof or to make general household repairs, even when she has saved quite a bit of money. In these cases, it is often not effective to show her that she has enough money to pay for the repairs, as she is likely to remain convinced that doing so is not worth the money.

The lack of success with a reasoning strategy is likely because the barrier is related to rigid behavior rather than to a lack of understanding. The facts do not in themselves drive the behavior. The saving of money can be a hoarding behavior. In this case, the individual hoards money rather than household objects.

One strategy can be to use a rule-oriented approach, convincing the individual to follow the "rules" of a budget. If she understands that the budget outlines a list of household items that should be repaired or replaced on a certain time schedule, she may be more likely to make the appropriate repairs. Similarly, a budget may include an annual amount that should be spent on household repairs and updates. Requiring a set amount may feel concrete, factual, and compelling to the ASD individual, thus making it logical to spend money on repairs.

Others with this tendency may have trouble with any change in their home environment and feel reluctant to replace the old, dirty, tattered couch with a new one. In this case, making small changes each year may be a good strategy. Perhaps the individual can learn to follow a schedule in which one piece of furniture is replaced each year in rotation.

Additionally, the individual within the spectrum may also get "stuck" in a state of indecision with lengthy researching behaviors and pondering of options. A common complaint of the ASD individual is that he feels "pushed" by those around him. Sometimes, the increasing pressure to make a decision seems to increase the stalling and "stuck" behaviors. This situation can be challenging, but in some cases, the individual will allow a family member to present two options to him, with the understanding that she must choose one.

This technique can be helpful because having a large, open-ended pool of choices can be very paralyzing for the individual with autism. It is much harder for her to consider an unlimited number of options across any life category ("What do you want to do tonight?") than a small number of options ("Do you want to watch the baseball game or read?").

Another approach to limit and structure the individual's indecision is to allow her thirty days to make a decision. If she is unable to make the decision within thirty days, a helper will present her with two options.

Likewise, if she is unable to choose from the two options within a certain time frame, the helper will choose. Adding some structure, rules, and reasonable deadlines may help the individual who is reluctant, stuck, or resistant to change. Family members may find that the difficulties remain, and therefore they "pick their battles" when choosing what changes to pursue in the ASD individual's household and what changes to defer.

Collecting, Hoarding, and Living in Clutter

Some ASD individuals live in a dirty, cluttered environment yet demonstrate too much structure and organization in other ways. For example, the individual who aligns the items on his chest of drawers exactly one inch apart and makes sure his soda pop cans face north may be the same individual with piles of clean and dirty clothes on his bedroom floor and a living room overflowing with books and electronics. One strategy in these cases can be to create some rules about space. The rules may depend on what the particular individual can tolerate. For some, a helper may be in charge of objects that the ASD individual cares deeply for, such as books and electronics. The rule may be that the individual can have ten of these objects out in his living space at any given time. The individual may earn another object for every day he keeps clothes off his floor by putting them in the hamper or dresser.

Another individual may not tolerate having her items doled out by another person. In this case, she and her helper can agree on where things go in the house, with the helper arranging labeled bins for certain objects.

The individual may have trouble visually searching for clothes in drawers and in the closet, and therefore prefers the clothes on the floor. In this case, the helper may buy bins that remain open for visual inspection, which helps the ASD individual find what he wants to wear each day while maintaining order in the living space.

When items have a specific place, there may be a rule that for every fifteen minutes she spends putting items in their assigned places, she earns thirty minutes of a pleasant activity. Another person may need to move some of her collections to storage units. This individual may earn one trip to the storage unit to look at her collection for every week that she takes a shower at least three times. Again, these strategies are not likely to eradicate the overall challenge, but they are likely to manage the issue in a more effective way than using verbal corrections such as, "I told you not to put your clothes on the floor!" Those aren't effective because they increase emotions and stress levels, which makes the situation worse for everyone.

Scheduled Tasks

To the extent that poor executive function interferes with general household tasks, a schedule posted in a visible place, such as on the refrigerator door, will help make chores predictable across the week since the individual will be able to see the schedule on a regular basis. It should divide larger tasks into smaller ones.

Each task on the schedule should be small enough that it does not exceed an effort level of 2 on a 1-to-5 scale where 5 requires the most effort. Although the individual can likely exceed a level-2 effort on one task, we are asking him to do several independent living tasks throughout days, weeks, and years. The goal is to pace the entire day and week so that the individual can have success in completing the tasks and sustain this in the long term. Some individuals in the spectrum prefer a visual schedule with pictures while others prefer lists with words. The schedule should be created using the individual's preferences and ability level.

Personal Hygiene: Too Much or Too Little

Personal hygiene should include washing the body, wearing clean clothes, brushing teeth, shaving, combing hair, and wearing deodorant. As with other qualities in the spectrum, attention to hygiene can be too focused or not focused enough.

Some individuals may wash their hands and body, brush their teeth, or change into clean clothes too frequently. When aides and medical staff understand why the behavior occurs, they can suggest appropriate interventions to keep the ASD individual from harming her skin, spending too much time during the day washing her hands or showering, or using too much cleaning product.

The following are the most typical reasons for why some ASD individuals engage in excessive hand and body washing:

- The individual may have a sensory over-reaction to the feeling or scent of dirt and sweat on the skin. Some individuals feel very upset about dirt or food on their hands, and want to clean them right way.

- The washing may be a repetitive or compulsive behavior that is separate from any concerns about feeling clean. Just as the repetitive behavior for one autistic may involve counting calories or graphing the weather, for another autistic the behavior may involve washing and cleaning.

- The individual may have an obsessive fear about germs or illness, leading to compulsions about washing clothes and skin.

- Some ASD individuals have fascinations with certain sensory aspects of the washing process. One person may be fascinated by the movement of running water, while another may be obsessed with laundry detergent including its scent and how the bubbles reflect light as the washing machine is filling with soapy water. In the same way that some autistic individuals are fascinated with parts of objects (such as watching a fan blade turning), some are attached to the sensory aspects of water and soap.

- It is also common for sensory-seeking behaviors to drive the urge to wash frequently. The ASD individual may feel calm in a warm bath because it provides the comforting sensation of deep pressure against the skin. Frequent soaks in the bathtub might be an effort to attain a sense of centeredness and calm.

In contrast, many autistics neglect personal hygiene. This may stem from a variety of causes.

- Some individuals in the spectrum have a sensory aversion to the feeling of shower water hitting the skin. Some have a dislike for the slimy feeling of soap or the scent of perfumed washing products. Many complain of the rough and itchy texture of the towels.

- The individual may show sensory under-reactivity and not realize she is dirty or has body odor. She may wake up in the morning with no sensation of discomfort in her mouth that compels her to brush her teeth. Likewise, this individual is likely to miss the fact that her clothes are worn, smelly, or wrinkled. The sensory experience of clean versus dirty may feel the same to some ASD individuals. When this occurs, the sensory drive that compels others to wash is absent. The individual may ask, "Why should I take a shower?" and complain that the activity seems pointless and unreasonable.

- As discussed earlier, the ASD individual may have poor executive function. In this context, he may be so fixated and focused on one task (a video game or jigsaw puzzle) that he is unaware of the need to do less compelling tasks, such as showering and brushing his teeth. He may have trouble with his own daily schedule and time management, realizing at the end of the day that many of his self-care tasks have gone unfinished. Likewise, if he has trouble with behavioral initiation, he may have difficulty starting a new task, including the redundant tasks involved in maintaining personal hygiene.

For the ASD individual who is under-reactive to dirt and scent or has trouble with executive function and time management, the most effective strategy may be to use a posted schedule to outline what task is done at what time. The schedule should list the small tasks that make up a larger task. This schedule can be written as a daily checklist so that the individual can check off the items as he completes them.

For example, a list can be written on a small dry-erase board that stays on the counter in the bathroom. When the individual is getting ready for bed, the following tasks can be checked off as they are completed:

- ✓ Take a shower
- ✓ Put on pajamas
- ✓ Brush teeth
- ✓ Use fluoride rinse

If the individual has trouble with behavioral initiation, it may be helpful for him to use sensory strategies to increase alertness and activation at various intervals throughout the day. A few examples of these are jumping rope, doing yoga poses, or swinging. The goal is to produce "wake up" sensations in the brain to give the individual a sense of physical and mental energy.

This can help him complete tasks during the day that otherwise would go undone due to his brain feeling sluggish and under activated.

For the individual in the spectrum who is so over-reactive to the environment that she avoids hygiene activities, the tasks themselves may need to be altered. For example, some individuals who dislike brushing their teeth can tolerate a vibrating toothbrush.

Others compromise by chewing gum during the day and then swishing/gargling with a fluoride rinse rather than using toothpaste and a toothbrush. Some who dislike the feeling of shower water pelting their skin feel soothed in a bathtub because of the warm deep pressure it gives. Others can only tolerate using a washcloth or baby wipes to wash their skin. The use of an extra soft towel, or wrapping the body in a cushy bathrobe instead of a towel, can also help some individuals tolerate the process of drying the skin after a bath or shower.

For the person who washes too much, a diversion of energies may benefit. For example, there may be a rule that they can take two showers a day and wash one load of clothes a day, but in exchange, perhaps they can do washing activities for charity at a shelter. Or perhaps they could be diverted to wash the car or the kitchen floor rather than re-washing the same thing over and over again. These diversions attempt to protect the individual's skin from over washing and to transform the repetitive behavior into one that has purpose.

Utilizing strategies of deep pressure can be comforting when the individual experiences the compulsion to wash. For example, an individual may be able to squeeze a stress ball instead of washing her hands. Another may be able to swing in a hammock for ten minutes to receive a state of calm instead of acting on the compulsion to wash repeatedly.

Sensory strategies can also replace some of the reward of the washing activities. For example, for the individual who feels calm in the hot shower, adding regular deep pressure and proprioceptive inputs (see sensory processing chapter) can add calm during the day in ways other than washing. Additionally, rewards can be worked into the mix. For the person who washes too much or too little, a reward can be given when the schedule is followed and improvements are made.

Food Preparation and Nutrition

The area of nutrition can be a struggle for some individuals in the autism spectrum.

- Some ASD individuals with sensory processing deficits in the area of interoception (what is going on inside the body) may not reliably know when they are hungry or full, which can lead to over or under-eating.

- Certain individuals with autism lack the behavioral initiation to actually get up and fix themselves something to eat, even if they will eat whatever is placed in front of them. These individuals generally show behavioral initiation problems in other areas of daily functioning such as hygiene or household chores.

- Many have repetitive eating habits that mirror other aspects of repetition in their lives. This may mean that they eat only familiar foods and may have a strict routine such as eating the same thing for breakfast, lunch, and dinner every day. Some may go on "food jags" where all they eat is refried beans for three months, and then they eat only hot dogs for a span of time.

- Sensory aversions may prevent the autistic individual from preparing or eating a wide variety of foods. Some are very sensitive to the textures of various foods. Others may seek certain food experiences like crunching on nuts or drinking a thick, cold smoothie through a straw. Aversions to food preparation and cleanup are also common, including disliking getting their hands sticky or slimy. They may also have an aversion to the smells that emanate from cutting onions, garlic, or raw meat, for example, and from the smell of food cooking, or the smell of discarded foods.

- Some individuals in the spectrum have extremely rigid beliefs about food, which can lead to nutritional and health problems. Tony Attwood, a psychologist in Australia and the author of many books on Asperger's syndrome, notes that some in the spectrum develop special interests around foods, counting calories, and rigid diets. This may be more common with girls in the spectrum. In his experience, up to 20 percent of female anorexics are also in the autism spectrum.

Interventions in the area of food and nutrition will depend on the characteristics and needs of the individual. The person in the spectrum who does not notice hunger or does not stop what he is doing to initiate preparing or obtaining food likely needs a daily schedule and perhaps alarms set to cue a change in task. In the case of someone with food aversions, changes to diet often have to fit within the specific types of foods the individual will eat. For example, if the individual will only drink smoothies, the intervention may focus around adding more nutrition and variety to the smoothies. Although an individual with ASD often has the uncanny ability to detect small changes in food, it may be possible to add a nutritional powder or liquid to the smoothie.

If another individual insists on eating the same thing every day, an intervention may include adding some vitamin gummies or perhaps small variations to one meal, adjusting slowly over time. Using gloves to prepare food may help the individual avoid touch aversions. Likewise, microwave meals or cold sandwiches may be preferable because they produce less of an odor than foods cooked on the stove. Creativity and small adjustments are often more successful than trying to change the overall eating habits or aversions of the individual, or relying on nutritional facts or reasoning.

Purchasing Household Goods

The ASD individual may need guidance and organizational help purchasing necessary household and personal items. Some have the tendency to lose track of what they have or don't have, sometimes purchasing too much of one item and not enough of another, such as thirty rolls of paper towels and one roll of toilet paper.

Individuals in the spectrum often have strong preferences regarding the brand and type of item purchased. Therefore, when their brand is out of stock, they may be unwilling or unable to make adjustments by purchasing another brand. For instance, they may eat a certain brand of ravioli every day for dinner, but when the brand is not available, they purchase no food and choose to skip dinner that night.

These individuals often benefit from using a budget to understand and recall what items are non-negotiable, what items are negotiable, and what items are luxuries. This helps them learn to buy food in advance before spending money on a special interest item that feels more compelling in the moment.

Some ASD individuals may go to the store and have difficulty with the wide array of choices available. This may cause them to feel flustered and scattered, and as a coping mechanism, they stay in one area of the store and come home with bags of pickles and olives but nothing else. Others may avoid stores because they dislike crowded spaces. For these individuals, sensory calming strategies before and after a trip can support their ability to stay in the store long enough to make appropriate food choices. It also helps to make a list in the exact order of where the items are located in the store, aisle by aisle. Alternatively, they may use online shopping to avoid the crowded store. Some stores allow you to place your order online and go to the store to pick up your items, thus eliminating the stress of grocery shopping altogether.

Transportation

Driving is another independent life skill that individuals in the spectrum may have difficulty with.

- Some ASD individuals I work with report that they don't like driving because so much visual information comes at them so quickly, which makes them feel anxious. These individuals may feel relaxed while driving quiet residential streets but anxious when driving on freeways or city streets, as well as when navigating unfamiliar areas.

- Many also feel unsafe with the unpredictable nature of all that can happen on the road (someone cutting them off) and the unexpected changes that can occur with their route or weather conditions. For example, I have worked with patients who were injured in accidents when they panicked after a missed exit or after needing to take a detour from their usual route. Other patients were injured in accidents because they continued to "follow the speed limit" even in inclement weather rather than reducing their speed. In their minds, they were following the rules as posted on the speed limit signs.

- An individual with ASD who has time management difficulties may also get into trouble while driving. He may run late for class or work, which causes anxiety about getting into trouble, letting people down, or breaking the rules. This anxiety can lead to speeding tickets or accidents, which adds points to his license, puts financial strain on his budget, and causes him to lose his car insurance or face a massive rate increase. Another ASD individual may speed because of challenges monitoring how fast she is driving. This individual may drive too slow or too fast unless she is paying specific and close attention to the speed at which she is driving in relation to the flow of traffic around her. This individual would likely benefit from using her cruise control even on short trips within town.

Getting and Maintaining a Job

When thinking about employment, a good checkup of the ASD individual's strengths and weaknesses in terms of thinking skills and behaviors is helpful. I often like to determine the pattern of intellectual, memory, sensory symptoms, executive function, and academic skills, and use this pattern to give input about jobs that may work well or not so well for the individual.

For example, a job at a cash register in a busy store requires quick thinking, multi-tasking, math skills, and people skills. A job as an emergency room nurse is likely to involve a rapidly changing high-stress environment, odors and germs, and strong emotions from staff and patients as well as family members.

Making a living as an author requires not only high-level reading and writing skills, but may also include creativity, the ability to network and reach out to others about one's books, and the ability to create and stick to a writing schedule without prompting from others. Knowing one's strengths and abilities, as well as one's struggles and difficulties, is key to finding a good employment match.

Before the job search begins, the ASD individual often benefits from an extension of social skills training to include developing written communications (job applications, a resume, and a cover letter if required) and verbal communication skills to use during an interview. Practicing interviewing with the individual will help to solidify talking points the employer might bring up during the interview. The interview training can include verbalizing why the applicant wants to work for that company. The applicant should be able to identify his strengths and weaknesses. He may be asked to verbalize what he would do in a conflict situation or how he has solved a problem in a previous job.

Additional coaching in interview skills would include general information about attendance and dressing in a manner consistent with the job. For example, interviewing for a position as a church secretary may involve different clothing than interviewing for a position as a barista at a college coffee shop. The applicant should also be coached to shake hands and smile, and to have a few questions prepared to ask the employer about the job. Depending on the individual's needs, it may be decided that a job coach should attend the interview. (A job coach is trained to help individuals with disabilities to succeed at work.) Alternatively, a specific discussion of ASD symptoms might be appropriate during the initial interview to demonstrate awareness to the prospective employer of the individual's anticipated needs and to raise the topic of possible solutions.

Another part of successful employment includes initiating a good relationship with the employer. For greatest success, the employer will be willing to engage in problem solving, advocate for employees, and work with an occupational therapist or a job coach to help find an appropriate job for the ASD individual, facilitate communication with the employer, and proactively solve any job-related difficulties that arise. Alternatively, a family member, counselor, or other therapist may assume the role of advocate with the employer. These support persons can help the employer know how to communicate with the ASD worker in terms of preparing him or her for changes in the work environment and resolving difficulties with coworkers.

Aspects of the workplace that may be relevant to success include the following:

- **Workplace culture**: The ASD worker may need help understanding issues related to the workplace culture that a neurotypical worker might understand without specific guidance or explanation. Culture may include dress code, attendance, incentives, goals of the company, and behavior that is allowed or not allowed.

- **Communication**: How is information communicated to workers? What should the new worker do if she has a question? Who is the direct point of contact? The new worker may even have a mentor she can meet with regularly to check on issues of communication, performance, and acclimation to workplace culture.

- **Adjustment to change**: The ASD worker is likely to have difficulty with change, especially unexpected changes. The more notice the employer can give the worker about an upcoming change, the greater the likelihood of a successful outcome. Likewise, the worker may do best in a job setting with a high level of predictability.

Additionally, the supervisor or manager may need to maintain an ongoing dialogue with the ASD individual's occupational therapist or job coach. If there is an issue to be discussed, perhaps it is decided ahead of time that the worker, employer, and counselor will attend a meeting together about the issue. Problem solving can be introduced to the worker as a part of the normal culture at any workplace.

Individuals advocating for the ASD worker may want to become familiar with the Americans with Disabilities Act passed in 1990. The ADA requires covered employers to provide reasonable accommodations to employees with disabilities. Job coaches, community agencies for developmental disabilities, and lawyers can help families determine what the ADA can ensure specifically in the workplace for individuals with autism spectrum disorder.

Recently, major corporations have stated they are searching for ASD individuals to work in certain positions within their organization. This has to do with the strengths that many ASD individuals have such as enjoyment of repetitive work, a fine eye for detail, and a preference to work alone rather than on teams. Indeed, much of the success found in the workplace for ASD individuals involves close attention to the applicant's strengths as much as an acknowledgement of challenges or weaknesses.

Managing Finances

Managing finances requires basic math skills and the ability to plan and prioritize. Time management skills are important for knowing when bills are due in relation to one's pay schedule, and allowing for processing delays due to weekends and holidays.

The individual may need help understanding how to prioritize the money deposited from her paycheck, specifically, paying any bills that are due before the next pay period, and determining which expenses are luxuries or extras. Creating and following a budget is helpful. The individual should be able to consider not only immediate purchases but also insurance needs, retirement savings, and savings for emergencies.

- Those with ASD may struggle with financial management because of difficulties with prioritization, planning, and resisting impulse purchases, especially if those purchases are for items of special interest to them. In this respect, some can benefit from learning very concrete rules about budgeting, such as saving 10 percent of their income every month. However, if they are able to learn a rule-based strategy, they may need monitoring and input from others about when to make exceptions to the rules. For example, spending money to repair a leaking roof takes priority over depositing money into one's savings account for that particular month.

- Because of the frequency of uneven cognitive and learning profiles in the spectrum, math disability may also be present. It is important to understand the ASD individual's ability with basic math concepts and calculations.

- Balancing impulsivity with rigidity can pose problems for some ASD individuals. One may spend everything quickly, which of course is not good, while another may be miserly to the point of not completing important household repairs because of not wanting to spend money. This difficulty in flexing and balancing is often a problem in the spectrum and can interfere with financial management as well as other areas of functioning.

- Additionally, many individuals in the spectrum have difficulty understanding the motives of others. They can be taken advantage of in the area of finances, giving money away to unscrupulous individuals or those who prey on their naiveté when it comes to managing money. The ASD individual often has difficulty detecting what is likely to be a scam as opposed to a legitimate enterprise.

If the ASD individual shows difficulty with financial concepts and money management that cannot be adjusted with a budget and some education, he may benefit from assistance with finances. A lawyer or financial consultant can explain the various ways a family member or a support person can monitor the finances and manage their money. If the individual is unable to work and receives SSI (Supplemental Security Income) or SSDI (Social Security Disability Income) payments, it may be appropriate to assign a payee to receive and manage the payments.

Some individuals in the autism spectrum benefit from having a guardian. This person may also be the overseer of their finances. A lawyer should be consulted regarding other financial options such as the establishment of a special needs trust.

Guardianship

The transition to adulthood includes significant changes in legal responsibilities and rights.

Many families feel anxious about considering guardianship for their adult child with autism, while still worrying that certain responsibilities exceed the capacity of the individual in the spectrum. The individual is suddenly expected to sign legal documents, pay taxes, purchase insurance, consent for surgery, and sign for a mortgage loan. In addition, the individual is expected to advocate for himself if he has a need for community services. This often involves completing applications and initiating contact with support services and government agencies as needed.

An individual on the spectrum may have the ability to do all of these independently or none of them. Alternatively, he may have abilities somewhere in the middle. He may be able to pay bills on time but not understand long-term financial planning. He may feel comfortable speaking to his general physician at check-ups but shut down and become overwhelmed with more complex medical decisions or hospital stays.

An attorney can provide specific information about options for guardianship. This may include full guardianship or limited guardianship specific to the person, such as making decisions regarding healthcare and education, or pertaining to the estate, including the management of finances and assets.

Chapter 8

Mental Health, Addictions, and ASD

Individuals with autism spectrum disorder are known to be at risk for other mental health conditions including anxiety, depression, and sometimes psychosis. Some individuals in the spectrum also seem to be at risk for substance abuse. Because the symptoms of autism spectrum disorder can mimic other conditions or co-occur with other diagnoses, misdiagnosis is common. As with other areas of research, more studies are needed specific to the adult and geriatric patient. The following estimates are taken from the existing pediatric and adolescent studies.

Anxiety

Anxiety is arguably the most common and debilitating emotional symptom in the autism spectrum. Van Steensel et al. (2011) published a meta-analytic study on the topic of anxiety and autism, analyzing the results published within thirty-one studies of children and adolescents in the autism spectrum. The authors report that nearly 40 percent of children across these studies were found to have such elevated anxiety that their daily lives were significantly impacted.

Specific phobias were found to be most common at 30 percent prevalence followed by obsessive-compulsive symptoms at 17 percent, social anxiety and agoraphobia at 17 percent, generalized anxiety disorder at 15 percent, separation anxiety at 9 percent, and panic disorder at 2 percent.

The authors note that the levels of anxiety found in the autism spectrum are significantly higher than the 2 to 27 percent prevalence found in neurotypical children. In fact, excluding panic disorder, the rates of anxiety diagnoses in children within the autism spectrum were more than double those found in typically developing children and even higher than those diagnosed with attention deficit disorder or learning disabilities.

Diagnosis of a separate anxiety disorder in autism can be problematic because of symptom overlap between anxiety and core autism spectrum features, such as rigidity of behaviors, repetitive behaviors, and obsessive behaviors. For this reason, some of the authors of the thirty-one studies used a measurement developed for the ASD population, or they adjusted the measures by excluding behaviors that overlapped with those in the autism diagnostic criteria. However, even these authors reported a prevalence rate for anxiety disorders ranging from 31 to 50 percent, which does not deviate from the overall estimate reported in the meta-analysis.

Although it is true that anxiety symptoms are often inherent in the autism spectrum, some authors (Ruta et al. 2010) have found common differences in the obsessions of children in the spectrum as compared with those with more classic obsessive-compulsive disorder (OCD). The ASD group tended to show obsessions with hoarding, ordering, and repetition.

The OCD group overall exhibited more severe obsessions and compulsions than the ASD group, and more frequent difficulties with thoughts and worries about aggression (being fearful of or imagining violence toward themselves or others) or contamination from germs or harmful substances, as well as compulsive checking behaviors, such as checking that the lights are off.

Additionally, van Steensel's meta-analytic studies found that obsessions and compulsions in ASD children began very young, whereas classic OCD generally emerged in older children. Some studies also suggested that the repetitive and ritualistic behaviors in ASD children tend to decrease somewhat with age, although this decrease was not consistently found across studies.

It was further emphasized in the meta-analytic report that neurotypical individuals may experience social anxiety in some settings but not in others. An example of this would be anxiety about speaking to a group of people but having no anxiety about mingling with a group at a party, whereas the ASD individual generally shows more pervasive symptoms across all contexts. Additionally, the neurotypical individual with social anxiety disorder can generally demonstrate adequate social skills and does not show the deficits in social communication and interaction in early development that are so characteristic of the ASD individual.

Depression

According to a meta-analytic review by Stewart et al. (2006), the prevalence rate of depression in autism spectrum disorder is somewhat difficult to measure, and studies report a wide range of results. Nevertheless, there is the suggestion that depression is higher in the ASD groups than in control groups. One barrier to obtaining good measurement of depressed mood in the autism populations is the overlap of symptoms between autism and depression. That is, the neurologic presentation of autism can include symptoms of limited emotions in the face or voice, social withdrawal, limited hygiene, and sleep disturbance, all of which are also typical of chronic depression.

It has been argued that this overlap of symptomatology can either wrongly increase the diagnosis of depression in this population or wrongly mask true depression in ASD individuals.

Asking the autistic individual to describe his emotions can yield limited information, and many studies have relied on family members to report what appears to be depressed mood. Many ASD study participants self-reported a low frequency of actual depressed mood. More frequently, reports of symptoms included reduced self-care, decreased interest in typical activities, and increased maladaptive behaviors such as aggression, opposition, and self-injury, the latter of which can range from severe (cutting) to mild (skin picking). It is known that autistic behaviors in general can increase when the individual is stressed or challenged in some way, whether emotionally, physically, or psychologically.

Based on another study that interviewed mothers of autistic children and adolescents, 14 percent rated suicidal thoughts or actual attempts at suicide as either currently present in their autistic child or very frequently a problem. This was compared with only 0.5 percent for children whose development fit the norm, and 43 percent for depressed children. The severity of autistic symptoms and overall intellectual levels did not impact the frequency of ideation or attempts at self-harm.

Ghaziuddin et al. (2002) reported that depression is most often described in teens and young adults within the spectrum. Depressive symptoms also appear to be connected with a worsening of other autistic symptoms including obsessive-compulsive behaviors, which may involve ruminations and repetitive thoughts about morbid topics. Some researchers have found that younger children in the spectrum who are depressed can present with impulsive and distractible behavior before puberty and more classic depressive symptoms during adolescence.

Additionally, ASD individuals who have functional intellectual levels may have enough insight to evaluate themselves negatively as compared to their peers, leaving them with a low sense of self-worth and a predisposition to depression.

Alcohol and Drug Abuse

The individual with ASD may be at risk for alcohol or drug abuse for a variety of reasons. First, many desire some connection with others but have significant social anxiety. They may report that social drinking helps them feel calmer and more at ease when interacting with others, and it may also help to diminish their obsessive thoughts. Similarly, marijuana seems a substance of choice for those seeking a sense of calm to supplant the anxiety that is so often prevalent for those in the autism spectrum.

It is important to note that individuals in the autism spectrum may be at risk for overusing alcohol or drugs because they seek repetitive actions and experiences.

However, research quantifying substance use in autism spectrum disorders is limited, but many clinicians note that ASD individuals tend to stay away from substances that create intense or unpredictable experiences. In addition, they are more likely to use substances that are easily accessible in their communities, including pain-reducing or sedating medications prescribed by their physicians. It is hypothesized that the ASD individual is less likely to venture far from home or enter parts of the community that are scary or unfamiliar.

Patient Scenario: Mr. Z

Mr. Z was a fifty-four-year-old gentleman who had always been considered "different" by his relatives and family friends. He had been able to hold a job as a machinist throughout his adult life, and he lived alone in a small townhouse that belonged to his family. When I met him in the hospital, it was while he was eating breakfast. He explained that his strategy for eating breakfast included chewing each bite fifty times. His first-grade teacher had given him this instruction, and he had faithfully done it at every meal ever since.

The reason he was hospitalized had to do with alcohol abuse. Six months prior to admission, he had a tooth extracted. It developed a dry socket with significant pain. Someone suggested to him that a swig of alcohol could relieve the pain and possibly kill bacteria and help with healing.

Mr. Z took this advice to heart. According to everyone we spoke to who knew him well, he had never been one to drink with any frequency prior to the last six months. Once he began that behavior, he never stopped. Indeed, he was drinking instead of eating, and was admitted with a brain injury resulting from this habit, an injury that affected his ability to walk and made it difficult for him to think clearly.

Psychosis

The presence of a psychosis is diagnosed when an individual has difficulty ordering thoughts coherently and distinguishing between reality and subjective experiences. The individual often has unusual experiences such as hallucinations (auditory or visual) and/or delusions (beliefs that are firmly held but are clearly false and are not accounted for by a person's culture or spiritual beliefs).

Historically, similarities between schizophrenia and autism have been described including symptoms of social withdrawal, limited facial emotion, lack of hygiene, and unusual beliefs. Schizophrenia is a psychotic disorder that typically emerges in young adulthood. Childhood schizophrenia is considered rare, and when present, it tends to occur before the age of twelve.

Although it is possible for an individual to have both disorders, clinicians feel that the conditions can generally be distinguished. Aside from schizophrenia, however, individuals in the autism spectrum may be at risk for psychotic features or brief episodes of psychosis during particularly stressful periods. Some have noted a specific vulnerability during adolescence. This is possibly associated with increased social pressure, school demands, and biochemical changes within the body.

It can be quite difficult to diagnose delusions in the ASD individual because doing so requires the ability to distinguish a delusion from the typically pervasive fixed and rigid beliefs held by individuals in the spectrum. For example, an ASD individual may believe that she is allergic to water because she has stomach cramps when she drinks water. She may refuse to drink water despite knowing that water is crucial to life. You can see where this belief may have come from, although its rigid nature is very difficult to break through using logical reasoning.

Alternatively, an individual with schizophrenia may also refuse water, but explain that it is because the national news anchor has tagged her water with radioactive material to read her thoughts. This is more clearly a psychotic delusion without any basis in reality, whereas the ASD individual's explanation lies within her rigid beliefs.

It is common for individuals with autistic qualities to attach significant meaning to things that aren't important to neurotypical individuals, such as colors, prime numbers, and the symmetry of shapes. For example, a woman with ASD may wear a red scarf because she has always had a deeply held feeling that red is a very important color. She has recently noticed that a man she finds handsome often wears a red tie. She tells her counselor that this means she and the man are destined to be together forever.

The difficulty this woman has in reading social situations and cues may contribute to her misreading of the man's intentions, causing her to believe that he is deliberately showing a romantic interest in her by wearing a red tie instead of simply having a preference for that tie or possibly owning a few ties, thus wearing the red one in frequent rotation. Her conclusion about the man's interest in her could be misinterpreted by others as a romantic delusion rather than the unusual and fixed belief that is part of ASD.

Misdiagnoses

Although autism spectrum disorder co-occurs with other mental health conditions, it is common for individuals in the spectrum to be given multiple mental health diagnoses before obtaining the more correct diagnosis of ASD, which encompasses the symptom picture as a whole. Although this list is not all-inclusive, I have personally seen the following diagnoses misapplied to adult and geriatric individuals in the autistic spectrum:

- **Schizoaffective Disorder or Bipolar Disorder**: This diagnosis may have been given if the individual displays strong emotional fluctuations, outbursts, and meltdowns along with symptoms that appear to be psychotic features such as lack of hygiene, non-normative fixed beliefs, or suspiciousness of others.

- **Schizophrenia**: This diagnosis may have been assigned due to lack of hygiene, unusual fixed beliefs, suspiciousness of the motives of others, unresponsiveness to external input, lack of social relationships, and possibly even brief psychotic reactions.

- **Paranoid Personality Disorder**: This diagnosis may be given if the individual has demonstrated a suspiciousness of the motives of others.

- **Schizoid or Schizotypal Personality Disorder**: These diagnoses are made in individuals who demonstrate features of social isolation and unusual fixed beliefs.

- **Narcissistic Personality Disorder (or Conduct Disorder)**: This diagnosis may be mistakenly assigned to the ASD individual because of limited consideration of the differing viewpoints of others and an overall pattern of black and white thinking. Both the ASD and narcissistic individual may have difficulty admitting when he is wrong, and may take a brusque interaction style with others, lacking empathy for the reactions of the listener.

- **Antisocial Personality Disorder**: This diagnosis may have been assigned if there is a history of substance abuse and emotional outbursts or behavior problems in the context of poor emotional control and self-regulation.

- **Borderline Personality Disorder**: Some ASD individuals may have been given a diagnosis of BPD because of significant mood swings, difficulties with sense of identity and self, and a lack of appropriate attachment to others (too close or too distant).

- **Avoidant Personality Disorder**: This diagnosis may be present because of social withdrawal, avoidance of social activities, and significant sensitivity to the possibility of interpersonal shame.

- **Dependent Personality Disorder**: DPD may have been misdiagnosed due to the tendency of some ASD individuals to strongly attach to supportive others such as family members rather than venturing out on their own.

- **Post-Traumatic Stress Disorder**: Individuals with disabilities are at higher risk than the general population for abuse and neglect than individuals without disabilities. This abuse history can lead to symptoms of post-traumatic stress disorder. In 2006, the Autism Society conducted a survey of over 1500 individuals in the autism spectrum and their caregivers. It was reported that 38 percent of those in the spectrum had experienced physical abuse or assault, 32 percent emotional abuse, and 13 percent sexual abuse. There are a multitude of reasons for this increased risk of abuse such as the increased strain on their caregivers, difficulties of the autistic individual understanding the motives of others, problems approaching others to communicate about difficult subjects such as abuse, and the higher prevalence of family members with developmental and intellectual disorders. When an individual presents with problematic behaviors and has a reported history of abuse, supportive others and assessing clinicians sometimes mistakenly attribute all of those behaviors to the abuse rather than considering the presence of a neurodevelopmental diagnosis, such as autism spectrum disorder. To summarize, a history of abuse should not lead us to assume that all behaviors are a consequence of the abuse.

- **Anxiety Disorder, Obsessive Compulsive Disorder, or Agoraphobia**: These may be diagnosed secondary to repetitive behaviors, obsessions, compulsions, social isolation, rigidity of thinking and behavior, difficulty with change, and generalized anxiety.

- **Attention Deficit Disorder**: ADD is a common misdiagnosis because of executive function impairment and sensory seeking behaviors among those in the autism spectrum. Although the diagnosis of ADD is not excluded in the presence of autism, it is often a way of labeling some of the core symptoms of autism without recognizing the whole syndrome of autism. As a result, it can serve as a misdiagnosis, thereby delaying the correct diagnosis of ASD.

- **Eating Disorders**: These have been diagnosed in some individuals secondary to rigid eating patterns and possible obsessions with counting calories or monitoring certain aspects of food and nutrition.

It is common for these diagnoses to be given because each captures a particular piece of the individual's overall demeanor and behavior. In the case of the ASD individual, however, there is a whole spectrum of symptoms, and Autism Spectrum Disorder is the diagnosis that encompasses all of the symptoms and correctly identifies the condition as developmental and neurologic.

Patient Scenario: Mrs. O

Mrs. O came to see me as an outpatient with a possible diagnosis of agoraphobia because her medical clinic realized she had so much trouble leaving her home that she was missing medical appointments. The more we talked about her history, the more autistic features emerged. Mrs. O was able to identify multiple sensory symptoms. "Sometimes I can barely take a shower," she explained. "It is so uncomfortable." She was tapping into the fact that her sensory perception could be more pronounced on some days than others. She knew that when this was the case, it would be very difficult to leave her home that day to grocery shop, for example, because that would involve coping with traffic and the oftentimes crowded and uncertain environment of the store with its bright lights, other shoppers' carts crowding her space, and the jarring noise of children crying. She knew that the stress of those situations would heighten her sensory processing difficulties, which were already misfiring that day.

When Medication Can Help

It is important to remember that medications do not cure autism, nor do they generally "fix" any particular symptom completely.

However, medications can improve an individual's quality of life and overall functioning, particularly when other strategies and supports are already in place. There are four areas of functioning within the autism spectrum that can sometimes benefit from medication:

- **Sleep:** As discussed, many individuals in the spectrum experience significant sleep disturbance, often with late onset of sleep, difficulty waking in the morning, and an overall disrupted sleep cycle. Medication or supplements for sleep may increase the individual's functioning during waking hours when he may need to attend work, school, community activities, or doctor appointments. Having better sleep can also improve the ASD individual's resilience during the day and lower adverse reactions to day-to-day events.

- **Depression or anxiety:** As discussed earlier, the ASD individual often presents with symptoms of anxiety and depression. Medication in addition to strategies to improve resilience can help with overall emotional comfort and engagement during daily activities.

- **Behavioral outbursts:** The individual with ASD often has difficulties with emotional control (identified as part of executive function impairment), self-regulation of her physical and emotional state, and over-reactivity to the sensory and emotional environment. Along with strategies to improve comfort, alertness, and resilience, medication may be used to decrease the frequency or diminish the severity of outbursts that otherwise might harm the individual's ability to maintain successful work and interpersonal relationships.

- **Attention:** Executive function difficulty is a core feature of ASD, and is often accompanied by sensory under- or over-reactivity. In this context, the ASD individual often has difficulty attending to the most important parts of her environment and letting go of distractions. The individual may be prescribed medication for attention deficit disorder. Some individuals in the spectrum seem to respond well to these medications, although it should be noted that the medication may improve attentional tone but is not expected to decrease sensory reactions or other symptoms that may feel distracting. It should also be noted that some medications in this class may increase anxiety and decrease appetite. These side effects can make the medication more of a barrier than a benefit. For this reason, the individual's response to the medication should be monitored.

The first and most important goal in treating the individual in the autism spectrum is to start with a correct diagnosis. This begins by understanding why certain behaviors occur, which in turn drives interventions for improved functioning. Once this understanding is in place, the goal is to set realistic expectations for the individual by creating a plan for adding appropriate structure to his or her daily schedule and living/working environment to increase comfort, engagement, and resilience while decreasing drain, loss of emotional control, and disengagement. Medications can add a final layer of support when other interventions and supports are inadequate to reach that goal.

Chapter 9

Healthcare

As of 2014, 3.5 million Americans were documented as carrying a formal diagnosis of autism spectrum disorder. Each of these individuals, in addition to the many who are undiagnosed, has specific medical needs throughout his or her lifespan. Despite the significant need, most medical clinicians who interact with adult and geriatric patients are unprepared and ill equipped to adequately serve those with autism spectrum disorder.

The results of a physician survey conducted by Kaiser Permanente Northern California were presented at the International Meeting for Autism Research in Salt Lake City in May 2015. The survey included responses from adult primary care, mental health, and obstetrics and gynecology professionals. Nearly every responder described lack of eye contact as a marker they would use to consider a possible ASD condition in one of their patients. Most under-reported the number of autism patients likely in their care, and only 13 percent of physicians reported having adequate tools or referral resources to accommodate adult patients with autism. Roughly 77 percent of clinicians rated their ability to care for individuals with autism as poor or fair.

Challenges in the Healthcare Environment

In addition to the medical professionals feeling ill equipped to serve the autism population, patients and families also report concerns. Dr. Bruce Wexler, Neuroscientist at Yale School of Medicine, notes in the Special Report on Autism in Healthcare (2015) that individuals in the spectrum and their families "routinely report negative experiences with the health system and concerns about the quality of care they receive."

The large number of individuals in the spectrum and the lack of knowledge and resources in the medical community are a two-pronged challenge when one considers that autistic individuals have a greater number of medical problems than neurotypical individuals. Specifically, the Special Report documents that more ASD individuals are diagnosed with chronic diseases than the general population. These include diabetes, epilepsy, digestive problems, high blood pressure, sleep disorders, and heart problems. Because of their higher comorbidity rate, children and adults in the spectrum spend more time in healthcare settings than the general population and accrue four to six times more in medical costs.

In "Comparison of healthcare experiences in autistic and non-autistic adults," Nicolaidis et al. (2013) state that autistic patients had greater difficulty communicating with providers, a lower sense of self-efficacy in their healthcare (a diminished sense of empowerment and the ability to bring about change), more frequent use of hospital emergency departments, greater unmet healthcare needs, and lower utilization of preventive services.

In her article "The Missing Generation," Jessica Wright (2015) cites the work of Dr. Joseph Piven, Professor of Psychiatry at the

University of North Carolina at Chapel Hill, who notes an unexpectedly high incidence of Parkinson's disease among adults with autism. He studied nineteen autistic adults over the age of fifty and found three with Parkinson's disease and nine with parkinsonian symptoms such as rigidity and tremor. A collaborator, Sergio Starkstein of Australia, described similar parkinsonian features in many of his adult ASD patients.

Lisa Croen, director of the Autism Research Program at Kaiser Permanente, found that adults with autism in her research group were thirty-three times more likely to have a diagnosis of Parkinson's disease or features of the disease.

Although some movement symptoms may result as a side effect from certain antipsychotic medications sometimes prescribed to reduce agitation in a subset of ASD individuals, even the patients who were not prescribed antipsychotics had a higher rate of movement symptoms than expected. Additionally, Starkstein found that some of his autistic patients seemed to be very sensitive to antipsychotic medications, and developed parkinsonian symptoms at very low doses prescribed over a short period.

Venkat et al. (2012) emphasize that the adult with autism can present to a variety of physicians' offices including settings for mental health, neurology, digestive or eating disorders, dental health, gynecology, and nutrition as well as primary care just to name a few. The authors encourage medical staff to be aware of the core features of ASD, the particular needs of their patients, and the possible adverse effects of various treatment approaches.

Aspects of Autism that Make It Difficult to Seek Help

Several features of autism are likely to interfere with adequate medical care and participation in a healthy lifestyle. Many ASD individuals have difficulty monitoring their internal states including hunger, pain, and fatigue. They may be over or under-reactive to internal physical cues and sensations. For example, some may not complain of pain until their eardrum or appendix bursts, while others are so hyper-attuned to normal bodily sensations that they constantly worry that a disease is lurking within their body. Some individuals with autism seem to seek high levels of internal sensations by consuming too much food or liquid. They may also have difficulty monitoring their body's needs, such as knowing when they need more sleep.

ASD individuals have difficulty with many aspects of executive function including planning and prioritization. This can mean there is a failure to make regular doctor appointments or to pick up medical prescriptions on time to avoid running out. Organization can also be a problem and lead to missed appointments or forgetting to eat regularly or take medication on schedule.

Rigidity in behavior can often lead to difficulty trying new health practices recommended by physicians, or stopping old behaviors to make changes in lifestyle and health. Even when rule-following approaches and schedules can be used to successfully introduce a new healthy behavior (the patient adjusts to eating fewer carbs), there may be difficulty helping the patient understand when to stop or limit the "healthy" routine (the patient begins eating mostly protein and avoids carbs altogether because they are "bad").

Executive function impairment in ASD is also associated with problems predicting likely outcomes that have never happened before. The individual may have a difficult time conceptualizing how an abstract concept such as "high cholesterol" puts her at risk for heart attack or stroke in the future. She may emphasize that no one can really know what will happen in the future. She may state that she feels no pain, and therefore knows that she is healthy. The tendency to use her current perception of health to make health decisions, rather than being able to take in new medical information to predict risks of future adverse outcomes, is often a stumbling block.

Difficulties with communication, including getting thoughts out and understanding the communication styles of others, can make the medical process quite a challenge. For the patient who has difficulty reading social context, understanding idioms and analogies, and interpreting nonverbal cues, a medical appointment can be a challenge. Add the sometimes fast pace of appointments and interactions with medical staff, and even more information can be lost or misinterpreted.

In addition, the adult patient is expected to initiate contact with his medical team to make appointments, report new information, and ask pertinent questions. The ASD patient who experiences social anxiety and has limited social approach skills may not contact his medical team even when he has a question or concern.

Some patients may report limited tolerance for the face-to-face communication of a medical appointment. These individuals may prefer email or some other form of communication. Likewise, because ASD individuals tend to have difficulty understanding the motives of others, they may reject new ideas presented by their medical team.

Some individuals in the spectrum have significant limitations to the range of foods they eat. Contributing factors can include the smell or texture of certain foods, and the tendency toward behavioral repetition and avoidance of change. ("I only eat eggs for breakfast. That is what I eat.")

ASD individuals are more likely to have food aversions than the general population, which can lead to a very restricted diet. The aversion may be based on sensory aspects or even the color of food. ("I only eat white foods.") Problems with restricted eating behaviors can lead to dehydration, vitamin/mineral deficiencies, constipation and digestive issues, and problems with blood sugar regulation.

Additionally, some in the spectrum seem to seek internal sensation by eating without stopping. They may even have a compulsion to procure and eat food without having a sense of when they are full. In these individuals, obesity, high cholesterol, and diabetes may become health problems. In contrast, others may have a significant preoccupation with various diets and spend a lot of time researching issues related to nutrition. These patients may expend a significant amount of time and energy counting calories or carbs, or, as noted previously, they may present with an eating disorder such as anorexia.

For those with disordered sleep cycles, it may be difficult to get enough sleep overall, and it may be problematic to interact with the medical team if the individual typically sleeps during the day. The inverted sleep-wake cycle can lead to missed appointments and lack of engagement in the community.

Strategies for Improving Medical Outcomes

The following recommendations can improve medical interactions and outcomes for the ASD individual, support partners, and the medical team.

ASD individuals are most likely to seek out medical attention in a familiar environment. It is recommended that the patient have a consistent core group of medical providers. To diminish social and sensory overload, allow the patient to come to a private waiting area rather than wait in a crowded room. To illustrate this, let's take a look at George's challenges and the strategies that helped him.

Patient Scenario: George

George was a fifty-six-year-old gentleman with an ASD diagnosis whose aging mother had developed new health problems and was unable to make sure George went to his doctor appointments. His primary care physician, Dr. Joe Garcia, realized that George would benefit from close connections with a few office staff now that his mother was less able to come to appointments. George was assigned one of the nurses and a case manager in the office.

Nurse Carol was always present at George's appointments. The case manager Julie was in charge of arranging specialist appointments, letting the new medical team know his needs, determining whether she could meet him at the specialist appointment, resolving transportation issues, and calling George to remind him of his appointments.

When George went to see Dr. Joe, he was immediately brought into "his" exam room rather than being asked to sit in the waiting room; the exam room did not change from appointment to appointment. Because George became attached to a few individuals, he felt comfortable coming to the appointment to see Dr. Joe and Nurse Carol because he knew they would take care of him. This made the management of George's high blood pressure and diabetes much easier than it had been the previous year.

As we saw with George, many ASD individuals benefit from knowing what will happen when they see a doctor. This is why consistency in the medical setting is beneficial. However, not all aspects of healthcare are consistent, and the patient will likely need to have a medical test or procedure, or see a new clinician at some point that will vary from her consistent routine of appointments and doctor visits. When this happens, the individual can benefit from practice and rehearsal.

- **Practice:** One form of rehearsal is actually doing a walk-through of the medical appointment ahead of time. The patient can be driven to the medical building and shown where he will check in. Next, he can meet the staff person who will take care of him at his appointment. This staff person can take him into the procedure room where he can see the tools that will be used to help him. He can be given information about his comfort, guided as to how he can ask for help, and prepped for what will happen after the appointment. He can also tell the staff what he thinks he might need that day.

- **Social stories:** A social story is a way to mentally rehearse a scenario before the actual event takes place. The story is given to the patient days or even weeks before her procedure so that she can read or listen to the story over and over as a means of preparing for the new experience. Social stories can be used for many daily situations including medical appointments, procedures, and new health recommendations, as well as situations related to school, work, or relationships. In the case of medical issues, a family member or a staff person can write a story about what will happen on the day of the procedure. ASD individuals who enjoy stories and creative writing may be able to construct their own stories when provided with relevant information.

Patient Scenario: Julie

Julie is eighteen years old. She has noticed that four new teeth are coming in, one on each side next to a molar, in her top and bottom teeth. Her mother tells her these are called wisdom teeth. Her new teeth are pushing against her other teeth and need to come out because there is not enough space for them to grow in like other teeth. Julie's sister Trisha had her wisdom teeth out two years ago, and reassures her that it will not be scary at all. Trisha helps Julia write the following social story to prepare for this big event:

Today is the day of Julie's appointment with the oral surgeon, and she feels a little nervous. She is not sure what to expect. Her mother takes her hand and walks into the office with her. They tell the lady at the desk that Julie is here for her appointment.

Nurse Emily comes to get Julie and takes her back to the room where she will stay for her procedure. Julie's mom says, "See you later, Alligator," and stays in the waiting room. The new room Julie enters smells like mint, and there is soft music playing in the background. Emily smiles and shows Julie around the room. Julie gets to see and feel the tools that the dentist will use.

Julie sits down in the chair, and the dentist, Dr. Pamela, comes in to say hello. Julie knows she will get medicine to fall asleep so that she won't feel any pain while the dentist pulls her teeth. The dentist asks her to count to ten, but she only gets to six before she falls asleep.

The next thing Julie remembers is waking up in the same room with her mother. "Hi, Julie," says her mother. "You are all done, and now you can come home." Julie is still sleepy and can feel cotton in her mouth, but she is glad she can go home. She knows that after she takes a nap, she and her mother will watch her favorite movie!

And that is what happened at Julie's dentist appointment—unless something unexpected happens, and that's okay, because Julia knows her mother is right there with her, and Dr. Pamela always takes good care of her patients.

Communication Strategies for Medical Appointments

Some individuals in the spectrum prefer to communicate in specific ways. Many do not feel comfortable with in-person contact or even talking with someone over the phone. Many may prefer emails or written communication. Ask the patient what her preferred mode of communication is, and use this to develop good communication strategies with her.

Individuals with ASD often need time to process information both during an appointment and after. They often complain of feeling "pushed" by medical professionals when talking about behavior changes and decisions that must be made concerning treatment. Allow extra time for the patient to take in new information. Ask him to repeat the information to check his comprehension, and allow time between appointments, if possible, for him to consider the changes.

It is important for medical professionals to understand that the individual in the spectrum is likely to have a concrete thought process. He is more likely than the typical patient to take medical instructions literally but be unable to abstract after the appointment as to when the instruction no longer applies. The patient may need very specific instructions as to what to do to improve his health, when to do it, and when to stop. Frequent check-ins with the patient can identify possible misunderstandings and risks that the medical team did not anticipate.

Patient Scenario: Mr. X

Late on Friday afternoon, I was called to see a patient being prepared for discharge. Mr. X was a seventy-four-year-old gentleman who lived alone. A few individuals from a local church checked on him regularly, and one had agreed to pick him up from the hospital and take him home. His medical team let me know that they were concerned about Mr. X because he had been walking the hallways for the last seven hours using his walker. They were unable to encourage him to sit down, eat, and rest. This behavior was new, and his medical team wondered if he had developed a medically related confusion that was leading him to pace without purpose.

When I spoke with the church member who came to pick up Mr. X, she mentioned that he had no family, lived alone in a small apartment, and often sent away home health workers because he did not like people coming into his apartment. She described what she knew of his history, and the details she provided included many autistic qualities. When I spoke to Mr. X, I walked the halls with him. As we walked and talked, he eventually stated that the doctor who had seen him that morning during rounds had told him that walking would help get his bowels moving. (Mr. X. struggled with constipation, and had mentioned that to the doctor.) And so Mr. X walked and walked and walked. He was now at risk due to fatigue from excessive walking, but also from not eating or drinking throughout the day.

I suspected that he had taken his doctor's advice literally, not understanding that he meant it as a general suggestion when he said Mr. X should walk regularly to improve his digestion and ease his constipation. Mr. X thought he was being "good" by complying with the doctor's order, while the physician thought he was providing general medical advice about a healthy activity that carried no risk.

In speaking with Mr. X, I avoided trying to reason with him about what I thought his doctor really meant. Instead, I explained that his doctor had just called me and let me know that it was time for him to sit and rest.

The next time we walked past his hospital room, he turned in with his walker and sat down on his bed. I sat in the chair in his room and chatted with him to keep him at ease while waiting to be discharged. His medical team learned that his concrete thought process impacted his interpretation of a simple suggestion.

Encouraging Behavioral Health Changes

Many individuals in the spectrum demonstrate great difficulty when instructed to change their behavior. They may make statements such as, "I'll need to think about that," or, "I'll decide when the time comes," but the time never seems to come.

The medical team may see more substantive progress with the patient if they encourage small steps over a period of time rather than large changes all at once.

It is also important to determine if some of the resistance to change has a specific source. For example, the ASD individual may refuse to change her diet because she has food aversions. If the team understands this barrier, they can choose a variety of healthy foods that the patient is willing to eat, thus working within the realm of what she is capable of doing rather than continuing to ask her to change something so dramatic that she is unable to make any progress at all.

Patient Scenario: Mrs. T

Mrs. T was a forty-seven-year-old outpatient who came to see me at the request of her medical team to help them manage some of her health conditions including her struggles with chronic pain. In the context of our discussion, she let me know that her son and daughter had autism, as did two of her grandchildren. They had accompanied her to the appointment and were waiting in a quieter area of the hospital. Mrs. T had multiple health problems including diabetes and significant arthritis. Prior to the onset of her arthritis, she had exercised vigorously and regularly, including two hours every morning and two hours every afternoon.

In discussing her history, it was clear she was in the autism spectrum, but had never been diagnosed. She mentioned that her diet consisted of mashed white potatoes. Sometimes she would have a teaspoon of seedless raspberry jelly for dessert, and she could occasionally tolerate a spoonful of peanut butter, and sometimes had a Slim-fast shake. She had attended diabetic nutrition classes and was trying to be a "good patient," as she put it, but no one realized how narrow her food choices were, and the resulting impact on her health, or why she chose to eat such a limited diet.

When I informed the medical team of Mrs. T's eating pattern, they were able to help her tolerate certain diabetic-friendly nutrition drinks. She also learned to add protein and fiber powder to her mashed potatoes, and to sometimes eat mashed cauliflower instead of potatoes.

Involving the Patient's Family or Support Persons

The most positive medical outcomes typically result from connecting the ASD individual, his medical team, and supportive individuals in his daily life. Involving others in the patient's health care plan is important to achieve communication goals and to understand what is happening outside the medical office. Support partners can provide key information to the problem-solving process and are often central to organizing and implementing new strategies at home.

Chapter 10

Resilience in Daily Routines

N ow that we have discussed the core features and associated symptoms of autism as well as the impact of autistic features on overall health and functioning, this chapter will focus on some suggestions to make daily life an easier, less problematic, and more enjoyable experience for ASD individuals and the people who love and care for them.

We must strive for increased awareness as we guide them toward a healthy, balanced rhythm in life. The more aware the ASD individual is about the reason or impetus for certain behaviors and reactions, the greater the ability to adjust his environment accordingly. When this approach is taken over the long term, she can start each day with a sense of purpose because she has a strategy that helps her feel capable, involved in life and society, and accomplished.

Key to understanding autism spectrum disorder is knowing what types of stimuli are difficult for the ASD individual and what types are grounding and soothing. If friends and family are aware that crowds and touch are difficult for the individual, she should not be asked to go to a movie and a dentist appointment in the same day. If deep emotion and new environments are difficult to manage, it is understandable that traveling to attend a funeral will likely feel overwhelming.

When you are interacting with someone who has autism, strive to be aware of his specific qualities and needs. Consider the following:

- What seems to fulfill him creatively, intellectually, and emotionally? What activities does he gravitate toward? What is soothing and calming to him?

- What is draining, irritating, or frustrating to her?

- Consider the demands of his environment. What steps must be taken to ensure his health, safety, and optimal daily functioning?

- What types of goals or motivations does she have?

- What demands are currently in place that are not a priority and could be removed?

- What support does she have to help her try new experiences and adjust to change?

- What ability does he have to learn strategies and eventually implement them on his own?

In addition to improved awareness of an individual's needs within the spectrum, approaching the daily routine with purpose and strategy is also important.

Daily Schedule

A specific structure for the day is often important for the individual with autism. Having a list of activities can be important to help those who have problems initiating tasks or who lack the internal drive to move from one task to the next. A schedule that pairs times with activities, or pairs the schedule with a visual timer, can help those with time management challenges.

A list of activities is also helpful for the ASD individual who has difficulty figuring out which tasks are the most meaningful or important and should be completed first, and which can be done last. The list can include activities that are a MUST and activities that are a CHOICE.

Schedules can take many different forms depending on the interests and preferences of the individual, and the demands of the day.

Patient Scenario: Jill

Jill was a fifteen-year-old student enrolled in special education classes. She had one schedule binder for school and one for home. Her school binder included pages for each day of the school week, and her home binder had pages for each calendar day. Every Sunday night, her mother sat down with her and helped her assemble both binders for the coming week. The schedule was a picture schedule including digital photos of her school and teachers, and clip art pictures. Jill could stick the pictures in her binder with Velcro. She could see what teachers she would work with in the morning and what classes she would attend in the afternoon. When there was an expected change in her schedule— for example, she would have a substitute teacher because her regular teacher was at training for three days—she and her mother changed her picture schedule accordingly.

The same concepts were used for her home schedule. In addition to routine tasks she had to complete such as hygiene activities and homework, the schedule included breaks. During the breaks, the schedule identified choices for both sensory activities and special interests. Jill felt calm and happy when she lay under a heavy blanket and used scissors to cut pictures out of magazines. She could earn extra fun time rewards by doing her MUST activities consistently.

Patient Scenario: Clyde

Clyde was a sixty-four-year-old retired draftsman. He loved the time he had spent making technical drawings and plans during his working years. Now that he was retired, he missed the structure and predictability of his work routine. He felt lost and without direction during the day. He wasn't completing his MUST tasks such as paying bills, or even his CHOICE tasks, which included reading. Clyde's daughter helped him develop a daily routine using technical drawing as a guide. To get him started, she sat down with him and helped him understand what MUST tasks were, how to split them up during the week, and how to make a schedule in the form of a technical drawing.

Clyde loved to draw out his daily routine, update it with any changes, and mark off each task as he completed it. Each day had one page and included some words and pencil illustrations within bubbles and boxes that were connected across the page. Whenever something unexpected happened, he stayed calm because he knew he could draw it into his schedule after the fact, which helped him see that it still fit into the picture for that day. He also loved the repetition of the drawing activity. Even though each day contained the same basic structure, he loved to draw and redraw each day, every day.

Filling and Draining Activities

In addition to developing a schedule to improve the initiation of important tasks and behaviors and to decrease anxiety associated with an "unknown" daily outlook, it is important to find strategies for improving the pacing of the individual's task completion throughout the day. This helps to prevent crises and meltdowns. Consider the image of a container being filled up and drained throughout the day. It is important to make sure attention is paid to balancing the filling activities with the draining aspects of daily life. The ASD individual may be filled up by watching YouTube videos, reading journals about birds, and swimming. He may be drained by noise, unexpected changes, or the strong emotions of others. Balance is important and can be improved with good monitoring and helpful strategies.

The first step to developing a strategy for an individual in the spectrum is to figure out what fills him up and what drains him. Make a two-column chart with one column labeled FILLING and the other labeled DRAINING.

Perhaps the individual can verbalize or identify what she loves to do during the day. Perhaps others around her notice what is calming to her and what she is drawn to. Put these events and activities into the FILLING column. Likewise, play detective to figure out what is draining for the individual. Perhaps dentist appointments, giving a presentation at work, or visiting certain family members is often overwhelming. Put these triggers in the DRAINING column.

Just as we all can experience the straw that breaks the camel's back in our daily lives, the individual with ASD may find that the "straws"—stressful triggers—are much smaller than they are for the neurotypical person, and the "back breaking"—falling apart, shutting down, melting down, loss of temper—is often more dramatic and longer lasting.

In order to develop effective strategies for self-regulation, it is important to pay attention to the larger picture of what leads to a loss of emotional control. For example, although an episode may be triggered when an ASD individual drives to work and discovers that his "usual" parking space has been taken by someone else, there is often a larger context to his frustration: difficulty sleeping, having a head cold, concerns about finances.

The way to prevent this small stressor from quickly and strongly tipping the scales is to make sure there are enough filling and calming activities to offset the drains.

Self-Checks

It is valuable for the ASD individual to monitor his own internal states. This can often be a challenging task, although with specific attention, improvements can be made. The internal states monitored may include emotions/stress, focus/calm, sensory inputs, and physical symptoms such as pain, sickness, and hunger. One individual in the spectrum may use a picture or color rating scale to determine how she is doing overall. Another may integrate pictures and words, or have some other number and word scale. The key is to creatively integrate the ASD individual's abilities and preferences.

Patient Scenario: Niki

Niki was a seventeen-year-old young woman with both autism and intellectual disability. She was able to learn to use a color scale to show "badness" or "goodness" in her internal state. The scale showed a calm blue on the bottom, which represented the good state followed by other colors that stacked up to the fiery red color at the top, which represented an upset, painful, or overwhelmed feeling.

Patient Scenario: Thomas

Thomas was a fifty-three-year-old businessman who was having difficulty keeping a level and calm head at work. He was developing a reputation for flying off the handle when a more reasoned approach would be best. Using the self-check technique, he was able to rate his state of calm five times throughout the day. He preferred to use a rating scale from 1 to 10 where 5 meant he felt just right, 1 was sluggish and unfocused, and 10 was about to explode. His goal was to be a centered person, with his rating somewhere around 5 much of the time.

Once he was in the habit of rating himself on the scale, he was much more aware of experiences and situations that helped him be more focused, stressed him out, or filled him up.

Calming and Alerting Strategies

Chapter 5 introduced sensory processing concepts including low registration of information (not noticing when someone enters the room; not noticing hunger or pain), high sensitivity to normal inputs (discomfort wearing certain fabrics; avoidance of salt and spice in foods), and sensation seeking, which can be movement based, such as swimming laps, or some form of internal sensation, such as overeating.

The detective work mentioned above includes noticing what inputs are upsetting to the ASD individual and what inputs are calming or focusing.

There are two kinds of sensory inputs to improve resilience during daily life: scheduled sensory inputs and crisis sensory inputs.

Scheduled Sensory Inputs

Part of the ASD individual's routine will include sensory inputs scheduled throughout the day between other activities. Let's consider William's day as an example.

Patient Scenario: William

William was a seventeen-year-old high school senior in the autism spectrum. He was in regular classes with a 504 plan that allowed breaks and other accommodations, such as extra time for tests. He was also working on becoming more independent. One goal was to make it to school on time, which had been difficult for him because he had significant trouble alerting himself and getting going in the morning.

The first part of his strategy for improvement was to use a sound alarm and a vibration alarm in the morning to wake up for school. He put the vibration alarm under his mattress and set it to begin vibrating in conjunction with another clock alarm. Being awakened with both sound and vibration helped him get out of bed on time. Next, he did twenty-five jumping jacks and took a hot shower to increase his alertness. He consistently ate protein and complex carbohydrates in the morning and drank water to get his physical energy going.

During school, he took two sensory breaks. The first one was scheduled during lunch. Eating in the cafeteria was stressful because it was too loud, so he ate his lunch in a quiet office wrapped in a heavy blanket while listening to music through his headphones. These sensory inputs were both calming and filling to him. Mid-afternoon, he took another break by jumping on a small round trampoline in the back of the gym for ten minutes and getting a drink of water. Chewing gum during classes helped him stay focused.

After school, he needed a full forty-minute decompression time. He ate another healthy snack and played computer games in his room. It was quiet there, and he could fully immerse himself in the gameplay. After this down time, he liked to walk around the pond in his backyard multiple times. The repetitive circling was both calming and alerting. Once he returned to the house, he did his homework in twenty-minute increments followed by ten-minute breaks. While doing his homework, he liked to breathe in the scent of peppermint oil to stay focused and calm.

After dinner, he played more of his video game, finished any homework he had left over, and started his bedtime routine. He did ten to fifteen minutes of yoga and put lavender oils on his wrists to help his mind and body calm down and drift into sleep more easily.

Crisis Sensory Inputs

When the regular sensory routine and scheduled breaks aren't enough, the individual will benefit from using sensory strategies to help with calming. The strategies should be planned ahead of time so the individual does not need to think about what to do in a crisis. Some ASD individuals benefit from having a section in their schedule binder that lists calming strategies. Although some of the strategies may be positive, calming thoughts, many will likely be sensory in nature.

William did well with his regular schedule and sensory coping strategies. However, when he had a very challenging day, he needed to have extra strategies to focus on. For example, one of the required classes at school was a speech class. Although the school team had accommodated his needs by adjusting the required assignments for him, they still wanted him to make two short speeches in front of one supportive peer and the speech teacher. William prepared himself for this challenge by knowing exactly which extra sensory inputs he would do before and after his speech to help him remain calm.

First, he used the rehearsal technique for his verbal speech, and he visualized a social story about the speech. After the speech, he would be allowed to spend ten minutes alone to listen to his music. However, on the day of the speech, he lost his notes and became extremely upset. He was afraid of letting the teacher down, he was afraid of doing the speech without notes, and he was afraid of the unknown. He began pacing the hallway.

A supportive teacher recognized this crisis moment for William and brought him to the office. The school counselor helped him take out his schedule binder and look up his calming strategies. One of his strategies was to blow air out of his lungs, exhaling slowly. After that, he breathed gently while silently counting to 100. He also used lavender oil to smell during this process to help him achieve a calmer state. After he counted to 100, the speech teacher was able to talk William through this unexpected difficulty. They were able to talk about this moment as one of those situations that are hard to handle but are not the end of the world. There were several solutions to the problem, but William and his teacher chose the solution that worked best for him so that he could successfully deliver his speech.

William and his counselor were able to talk about this event a few days later when William had recovered from the situation and distanced himself enough to stay calm despite the stressful memories it evoked. His counselor was able to help William recognize the cues he may have had that he needed to use calming strategies sooner. They talked about how his breathing got fast and his heart started to race.

His counselor suggested that the next time that happened, he should take out his self-rating page and determine where he was on his stress scale. In this instance, the self-check step could have shortened and lessened the stress crisis. William and his counselor decided to make this his next goal: self-checking and independently using coping strategies to help him through a crisis situation. They also discussed all the things William did correctly before and after he gave his speech to the class.

Chapter 11

Bringing It All Together

In this final chapter, as a way to review the information covered in this book, we will take a closer look at two case studies to illustrate the unique challenges and journeys of individuals with ASD. Specifically, we will examine how they learn to live independently yet in partnership with the people who love and support them.

As noted earlier, autism is a diagnosis that emerged in the 1950s through observations of certain behaviors in children during their early development years. In a formal way, the diagnosis was born in the 1980s as part of the DSM III and III-R diagnostic manuals. The description of symptoms necessary for a diagnosis has evolved over time.

Currently, there is one diagnosis that describes a continuum of features and severity, and that is autism spectrum disorder. Autism is a diagnosis of behavior and can be present with or without an intellectual disability. ASD is a developmental neurologic condition that is present across the lifespan, although most current specialists focus on childhood. There is a great need for accurate identification of autism in adults and aging adults. Correct diagnosis helps to eliminate inappropriate treatments, improve communication, and deepen understanding of an individual's needs. Diagnosis drives effective interventions and allows the ASD individual to qualify for services in the community.

Although some symptoms of autism are features we can all relate to ("I hate noise too" or "I fall apart when I have a hard day" or "I'm an introvert"), autism is diagnosed when multiple symptoms cluster together, are present in a significant or dramatic way, and lead to impairments in health, independence, and quality of life. Think of it this way: although we all experience forgetfulness, the dramatic memory loss in Alzheimer's disease is a real diagnosis, a real struggle, and a real public health problem. The same is true for autism. ASD is more than just a quirky personality or a preference to be alone. It impacts many individuals and families in very real and debilitating ways.

Good detective work helps drive effective interventions and supports for the individual in the autism spectrum. Knowing the strengths and challenges of each individual is part of the problem-solving process. Strategies for improving resilience, communication, coping, physical health, emotional regulation, and independent life skills are available and effective.

Case Study: Mr. York

Mr. York was an eighty-three-year-old gentleman who lived independently in an apartment. He had never married and had no children, nor any living relatives. He seemed closest to a female friend named Lois who had been a classmate and neighbor in his small town. Lois and her husband John had taken Mr. York under their wing, taking him out to shop for food, making sure he had a place to go for holidays, and checking on his living situation.

After several falls in his small efficiency apartment, home health physical therapists advised Mr. York to remove the throw rugs in his living space to improve safety. Neighbors reported that he was often seen pacing the narrow hallways of the building, or could be heard pacing within his apartment. Although this had been his practice for many years, his increasing age, the need for a walker, and the confines of his small apartment were making the walking harder and more dangerous.

Mr. York had not seen a doctor for twenty years prior to his most recent falling incident. His new medical team noticed several unusual things about his behavior. He used big vocabulary words and talked quite a lot. He was difficult to reason with and seemed to talk over people rather than conversing with them. He focused on his own opinion rather than taking in new information. When staff tried to redirect him back to the health topics they were discussing with him, he became angry very quickly. Sometimes he would shut down or walk away if the conversation took a turn he did not like.

At his doctor appointments, Mr. York paced with his walker, and would not take a seat when asked. He was restless, opinionated, and difficult to talk to. Many of the female staff complained that he made inappropriate comments to them that were either too familiar or sexual in tone. All the staff felt that he was irritable and often angry, and nothing they suggested or did for him seemed to be helpful or well received.

Staff also wondered if he was confused or delusional. He told stories about his childhood and his life that did not seem likely based on what they knew of his personal history. For example, he claimed that he had been the president of six large Midwestern companies during his lifetime, but his story didn't check out or mesh with other verifiable details of his life. Because of Mr. York's age, his medical team was concerned that he may have a form of dementia that would worsen over time. The team needed more information, including a better history of his past behaviors and abilities.

The medical team asked Mr. York if they could meet with Lois and her husband to hear more about his history and to review with Lois some suggestions for Mr. York's health and safety. Mr. York trusted Lois, and once she reassured him about the process, he said he would feel fine about that arrangement. He let them know he was done talking anyway, so John took him outside to walk while Lois met with the team.

Lois had known Mr. York for sixty-five years and could describe quite a bit about his history and recent status. She let the team know that his behavior was long standing, to a great extent, although he seemed to have more trouble as he aged. However, his memory and thinking skills appeared quite preserved. Lois described his memory as fairly sharp concerning day-to-day events, with no significant episodes of forgetfulness.

Lois said that Mr. York had always needed the oversight and assistance of his family. He had graduated from high school with Cs and Ds, and had never demonstrated expected levels of independent behavior for his age. He lived with his mother until her death and then with his aunt until she died. He worked for the family companies but only in repetitive, unskilled work cleaning and organizing the sales space. For financial reasons, the family had put his name on six of the small businesses to diversify ownership. He had been identified as the president of the businesses, and he seemed to feel that he had indeed served in that role.

After Mr. York's family passed, he inherited the money gained from selling the companies. He lived in the family home and used his inheritance for about fifteen years before the money ran out. He worked for about two years as a janitor at a church but had difficulty completing the work and staying calm. He eventually sold the family home for financial reasons, and moved into the efficiency apartment he still rented.

Lois noted that he had never had close relationships outside his family, and although he had been close with her and her husband, it was not really what she would call a friendship. He had always been considered "different" and had odd behavior. He held conversations with himself, repeating various themes and not allowing others to provide their opinions or inputs. When he met new people, he had a general "story" he told about himself that was accurate but repetitive. There was no spontaneity or variance in the stories he told about himself or his childhood. He was generally lost when others used nuances in conversation, told jokes, discussed abstract concepts, or laced their comments with sarcasm. He did not often change his mind about things or show an appreciation for the viewpoints of others.

Lois noted that Mr. York began walking ten miles a day about thirty years ago when his doctor suggested walking as a way to lose weight and improve his health. Once he developed this habit he was religious about following the instruction regardless of weather conditions. Rain or shine, summer or winter, he was never deterred from his daily walk. However, once he moved from his home to the apartment, the walking was more difficult. The building was on a small piece of land, the sidewalks were broken and difficult to navigate, and he didn't feel safe walking the neighborhood alone. As he aged, he was more reluctant to leave the apartment, but he persisted in his pursuit of walking ten miles in the hallway and in the apartment each day.

Lois enjoyed gardening and often invited Mr. York to help her. He had taken to this hobby, but now he was physically unable to handle the tasks involved. He did continue to go with his friends to flea markets and garage sales to collect his favorite items—vintage postcards and turtle figurines—but this was posing a challenge now that he lived in a small space. The piles of postcards and figurines took up too much space for him to navigate around them, and his friends had to store some of his things at their home. Mr. York seemed to tolerate this fairly well because he visited their home once a week. While Lois and John ate dinner at the dining room table, Mr. York preferred to take his meal on a tray so he could eat while he looked through his collections.

Lois noted that Mr. York had always been difficult to interact with, but his rigid preferences and his increasing physical difficulties were beginning to overwhelm her and her husband. They were hoping they could back away from some of the responsibilities they had taken on while remaining available for visits and check-ins.

Based on the detailed history provided by Lois as well as an evaluation by a psychologist, Mr. York received a new diagnosis of autism spectrum disorder. Because the medical staff now understood the root of his rigid and sometimes questionable behaviors, an appropriate plan of intervention was devised. After the helpful information-gathering session with Lois, Mr. York's medical team formulated a plan. His core team included Dr. Nate, Jen (a nurse), Ed (a social worker), and Caryn (a counselor). The team occasionally consulted with other medical specialists including a physical therapist, an occupational therapist, and a nutrition specialist.

The following plan was developed and utilized with the agreement of Mr. York and with the help of Lois and John.

Dr. Nate met with Mr. York for a thirty-minute session. Because Mr. York preferred to walk, the doctor walked beside him down the long, wide hallways of the medical building as they talked. Because a previous doctor had made the original suggestion to walk for improved health, Dr. Nate's goal was to introduce new advice to change this repetitive behavior.

To improve rapport, Dr. Nate showed Mr. York a postcard heirloom that his father had sent his mother while he was stationed in Europe during World War II. Mr. York was very interested in the postcard and noticed multiple small details about the card that interested him. Dr. Nate said he had another postcard he could bring in for Mr. York to see during their next appointment.

Dr. Nate told Mr. York that the new medical advice for his health was to walk three times a day for ten minutes. He let Mr. York know, however, that he also had some new exercises for him to do at home instead of walking. Understandably, Mr. York let his doctor know that he wasn't really sure about that change, but he did ask some questions about the new exercises and wanted to know more.

Lois reinforced the doctor's suggestions to Mr. York as she drove him back to his apartment. Mr. York knew that a friend of Dr. Nate's named Jo, a physical therapist, would come to the apartment and teach him the exercises. Lois showed him a picture of Jo and taped the picture to Mr. York's calendar to highlight the days of the exercise sessions.

Nurse Jen was identified as the person who would develop a phone communication schedule with Mr. York. At first, he knew she would call every Monday at noon. The conversation was also somewhat structured. First she would say, "It's your favorite nurse Jen," and he would say, "You're my only nurse Jen." She asked him simple questions about his comfort, sleep, and nutrition. The last thing she did was to invite Mr. York to ask a question or tell her something about his health that she hadn't known to ask. At first, he had trouble thinking of anything to say, or he would say something off topic or inappropriate.

Over time, however, the routine was so established and familiar that he began to mention new things. One time, he mentioned he almost fell when he stood up because of dizziness. This helped his doctor know that he may have orthostatic hypotension, a significant fall in blood pressure when moving from a sitting to a standing position. The physical therapist Jo was able to check for this during their exercise sessions, and the medical team had important new information about Mr. York's health and safety.

Ed was a social worker on the team who helped Lois search for a better living situation for Mr. York. This part of the plan took some time and involved a review of his resources as well as some funds that Lois and John were able to contribute if needed. An investigation started with a review of assisted living facilities and then branched out into considering duplexes with more space and a safer layout.

After about seven months, a duplex became available for a cost that Mr. York could afford. It was in a nicer neighborhood and had a better walkway, and was closer to Lois and John's house. Mr. York was given a binder with pictures of each room in the duplex and the outside space so that he could look at them every day to mentally rehearse what it would be like to live there. After a week of reviewing the pictures, he wanted to go see the duplex. Lois and John took him over and showed him the outdoor space that Lois would fill with flowers. They also introduced Mr. York to the other tenant in the duplex and showed him where he could store his favorite collectibles. Mr. York needed help with the specifics of the move, but he made the emotional transition more easily than Lois expected, partly because he seemed to like the space better than his apartment, and he appreciated having his postcards and figurines near him. Lois and John had the resources to hire someone to check in on him when they were unable to visit.

Caryn was the counselor who developed home strategies to improve health and safety. These included a visual schedule, sensory calming strategies, and ideas to help him enjoy his hobbies even though he was slowing down and less able to go to flea markets.

Caryn spent time with Mr. York and Lois developing lists of filling and calming activities, and activities that were more draining for him.

Filling/Calming Activities:

- Sorting and reviewing his postcard collection and ordering his figurines from smallest to tallest or by color

- Sitting on the porch to look at the flowers that Lois planted near the front steps

- Sitting quietly with soft music playing on the radio

- Walking and doing his exercises

- Reading

- Watching baseball on TV

Draining Activities:

- Meeting or working with new professionals or home health aides

- Not being able to see Lois and John as frequently as when he had lived in the apartment

- Changes in his environment, including a short hospital stay after a fall

Caryn helped Mr. York develop a visual schedule with daily activities grouped into two categories, MUST and CHOICE activities. For example, Monday morning had pictures of his morning hygiene activities followed by his preferred breakfast of coffee and toast. Once those tasks were completed, Mr. York had time to sort through his vintage postcards. At noon, the schedule showed a picture of nurse Jen to represent her usual check-in visit.

The next part of the schedule was a picture of lunch. Lunch was his choice of microwave meals that Lois and John had stacked in his refrigerator freezer on the previous Sunday. Following lunch, his schedule showed the arm and leg exercises that Jo had taught him to perform. In the afternoon, Mr. York spent time walking up and down his street. During the last lap, he stopped at the mailbox then sat on the porch to look at the flowers. His schedule listed dinner at 5:00 p.m., and this was provided by Meals on Wheels. After dinner on Monday, he liked to watch the baseball game on TV or read a book. His schedule then pictured his evening hygiene activities and taking his medications.

Each day's schedule was similar in core features, but different in some details. For example, on Tuesdays and Thursdays, his hired health aide came to visit and check on him at 2:30 p.m. On Sundays, Lois and John came over to visit and sometimes brought a new figurine or postcard. They stocked his refrigerator and organized his medicines for the next week. They also sorted through his mail to make sure the bills were paid on time. Appointments with Dr. Nate or others were also pictured on his schedule.

Mr. York adjusted to many of the changes fairly well, and his safety increased. Lois and John were able to spend less time helping him and more time taking care of their own health and family priorities. There were challenges along the way. Although

Mr. York walked less, he was never able to slow down as much as recommended by Dr. Nate. He did seem to like using arm and leg exercises to replace some of the walking. Once in the duplex, his environment allowed more safety for walking. However, he did continue to have some falls, and was hospitalized once for a fall, dehydration, and a broken wrist. He showed improvement with eating and completing hygiene tasks more regularly, although sometimes he became dehydrated because he forgot to drink enough liquids. Overall, Mr. York appeared to adjust fairly well to this "new normal" routine.

Mr. York's story highlights many of the topics we have discussed in previous chapters. For example, he was an aging individual who had lacked an accurate diagnosis before he began having increasing difficulties and lack of support at home, mainly after the death of his mother and aunt, who had lived with him and looked after him. He needed supportive individuals to help him structure his external environment, but with this structure, his living environment was safer, and he was able to adhere to health and hygiene activities with greater regularity. He also showed decreased anger and resistance to change. The use of a daily schedule, a predictable group of core people helping him, and a balance of filling and draining activities and events were key to improving his quality of life and medical outcomes.

Case Study: Tara

Tara was a thirty-three-year-old young woman with a master's degree in chemical engineering. Although she liked the structure and challenges of her university coursework, she had been disappointed to find her fellow students less intellectual than she had hoped. She had passed through her internship adequately, although her supervisors noted she had some difficulty thinking quickly on her feet, working in teams, and organizing herself to meet company goals.

She easily obtained work, and after landing her first job, she rented an apartment. Unfortunately, being successful at work was more difficult than being successful at school because her performance was judged on the basis of speed, multi-tasking, teamwork, and communication, not just academics. After two years, she was let go from her job. Comments from her employer were similar to those she had heard during her internship training.

Tara went through three similar positions, each time struggling to accomplish work tasks in a timely manner. She was not well liked by her coworkers, who considered her inflexible and aloof. She voluntarily left her last position after being placed on a level one disciplinary warning for consistently falling behind in her work. Her inability to succeed at work frustrated and worried her.

At the advice of her cousin, she sought counseling with a focus on social skills and time management. Tara's psychologist, Dr. Warren, performed a thorough history and assessment, providing her with a new diagnosis of autism spectrum disorder. They spent several sessions discussing what this diagnosis meant. Tara was initially resistant to the idea of having autism spectrum disorder, and argued with Dr. Warren every step of the way. Eventually, she saw the truth in the diagnosis, and even brought up signs and symptoms not identified in the original assessment.

Over the next year, Dr. Warren and Tara developed goals and strategies related to social skills and relationships, work success, and independent living. Because of her lack of employment, she first had to give up her apartment and move in with her mother, who was widowed and lived locally. This would allow her the time and financial flexibility to work toward improvements before trying another job.

The first focus of treatment was to develop a home schedule designed to teach Tara how to break large projects into smaller tasks, improve her time management skills, and focus on self-care and hygiene routines. The schedule included balancing goal-directed work with several rest breaks. The rest breaks were a balance of physical activity and things that Tara enjoyed doing, including reading scientific journals and watching classic films.

Tara seemed to make some progress in her home functioning during the first three months of treatment. She was more attentive to her bathing schedule, and she was beginning to catch on to using physical activity to regulate her focus. She had made progress in taking on smaller daily goals as she worked toward completing a larger project. Her next steps were to improve speed of task completion, not get stuck in details, and stick to her scheduled breaks.

After Tara had made progress with these basic strategies at home, and was demonstrating an understanding of the social skills she was practicing, Dr. Warren suggested she use some of those skills in her local community. She signed up for a film appreciation class at the local community college and began two hours of weekly volunteer work at a local theater. This was challenging for her, but these challenges provided the opportunity to work on balancing her needs even when her schedule was busy.

As part of her work for the film class, Tara met some other students interested in film. Through this connection, she was invited to take a part-time job at a local film theater that specialized in art films and classic movies. Although this was a far cry from her original goal of a full-time engineering job, she felt she was making progress toward her goal of independence without overcommitting her time and energy.

Returning to a work environment was more challenging than she had anticipated. The many new things about the environment took some getting used to, and she had to work harder to make sure she had enough recovery time and sensory breaks. As the days settled into a familiar routine, she found comfort in the structure and felt more confident in her ability to manage her own reactions to unexpected events.

After working at the theater for six months at twenty hours a week, she increased to thirty hours weekly. Her work environment was less demanding and fast paced than her previous engineering jobs, and because she only had a few coworkers, she was able to forge better working relationships with them.

Tara also increased her social connections by joining an online community devoted to topics around film. As part of her interactions online, she developed a connection with Paul, a fellow film devotee. Paul lived about two hours away, and eventually Tara and Paul met in person. They enjoyed each other's company and were content with frequent online contact and less frequent in-person interactions.

At the end of a two-year period, Tara was able to rent what had originally been a small guesthouse on the property of a wealthy older woman in her community. The rent was low because Tara also tended the woman's garden, an activity she found relaxing and enjoyable. She continued working twenty to thirty hours a week at the theater and enjoyed her interactions with Paul.

Tara and Dr. Warren both agreed that the journey toward change had been successful for her. She was happy now, and more attuned to her strengths and challenges. She lived modestly and was financially self-reliant. She had developed a small circle of friends that she enjoyed.

The lives of Mr. York and Tara opened up to new vistas of happiness, safety, and wellness when they were each given an accurate diagnosis of autism spectrum disorder. Though they were in different seasons of life, they strove toward better health, quality of life, and independence. The diagnosis of autism was integral to developing successful steps to move forward and make steady progress in their daily lives.

Afterword

Thank you for taking the time to read this book to learn more about adults with autism spectrum disorder. I encourage you to recognize and support the strengths and challenges of ALL individuals in the autism spectrum, regardless of sex, age, or their particular patterns of strengths and challenges.

When we fully understand that behavior is connected to brain functioning and not just to motivation, commitment, and determination, we will truly be able to help every individual succeed according to his or her unique abilities.

All communities will benefit from improving the quality of life, physical health, relationships, and workplace independence for individuals with the autistic challenges of social connection and flexible behavior.

I invite you to join me in this endeavor.

Theresa Regan

Endnotes by Chapter

Chapter 1

Brugha, Traolach S. et al. "Epidemiology of autism spectrum disorders in adults in the community in England." *Archives of General Psychiatry* 68.5 (2011): 459-465.

Baron-Cohen, Simon et al. "Prevalence of autism-spectrum conditions: UK school-based population study." *The British Journal of Psychiatry* 194.6 (2009): 500-509.

Kim, Young Shin et al. "Prevalence of autism spectrum disorders in a total population sample." *American Journal of Psychiatry* 168.9 (2011): 904-912.

"The missing generation | Spectrum - Autism Research News." 2015. 15 Jan. 2016 <https://spectrumnews.org/features/deep-dive/the-missing-generation/>

"Girls and women who have Asperger's - Tony Attwood." 2013. 15 Jan. 2016 <http://www.tonyattwood.com.au/index.php/about-aspergers/girls-and-women-who-have-aspergers>

Gerhardt, Peter F. "The current state of services for adults with autism." *Advancing futures for adults with autism: Think tank* (2009).

Chapter 2

"IQ and School Achievement | Education.com." 2009. 16 Jan. 2016 <http://www.education.com/reference/article/iq-school-achievement/>

"Why g Matters - University of Delaware." 2015. 16 Jan. 2016 <https://www.udel.edu/educ/gottfredson/reprints/1997whyg matters.pdf>

"Dyspraxia and autism spectrum disorders - NAS." 2010. 8 Nov. 2015 <http://www.autism.org.uk/about-autism/related-conditions/dyspraxia/dyspraxia-and-autism-spectrum-disorders.aspx>

Gail Williams, P., Lonnie L. Sears, and Anna Mary Allard. "Sleep problems in children with autism." *Journal of Sleep Research* 13.3 (2004): 265-268.

Goldman, Sylvie et al. "Motor stereotypies in children with autism and other developmental disorders." *Developmental Medicine & Child Neurology* 51.1 (2009): 30-38.

Chapter 3

Wang, Z. "Capturing Complex Spatio-Temporal Relations.... - ECSE." 2015. <http://www.ecse.rpi.edu/~cvrl/zihengwang/papers/cvpr2013.pdf>

Kracke, IIse. "Developmental prosopagnosia in Asperger syndrome: presentation and discussion of an individual case." *Developmental Medicine & Child Neurology* 36.10 (1994): 873-886.

Stewart, M. E. "Emotional recognition in autism spectrum conditions from...." 2013. <http://aut.sagepub.com/content/17/1/6>

de Marchena, A. "Conversational gestures in autism spectrum disorders...." 2010. <http://geniiz.com/wp-content/uploads/sites/12/2012/01/13.pdf>

Kohen-Raz, Reuven, Fred R. Volkman, and Donald J. Cohen.
"Postural control in children with autism." *Journal of Autism
and Developmental Disorders* 22.3 (1992): 419-432.

Rinehart, Nicole J. et al. "Gait function in newly diagnosed
children with autism: cerebellar and basal ganglia related
motor disorder." *Developmental Medicine & Child
Neurology* 48.10 (2006): 819-824.

"CDC | Signs & Symptoms | Autism Spectrum Disorder
(ASD...." 2009. 12 Nov. 2015
<http://www.cdc.gov/ncbddd/autism/signs.html>

Laugeson, E. A. "Evidence-based social skills training for
adolescents with...." 2012.
<http://www.ncbi.nlm.nih.gov/pubmed/21858588>

Reichow, Brian, and Fred R. Volkmar. "Social skills
interventions for individuals with autism: Evaluation for
evidence-based practices within a best evidence synthesis
framework." *Journal of Autism and Developmental Disorders*
40.2 (2010): 149-166.

Chapter 4

Peg Dawson and Richard Guare, *Smart but Scattered* (Guilford
Press, 2009).

Chapter 5

Tomchek, Scott D., and Winnie Dunn. "Sensory processing in
children with and without autism: a comparative study using
the short sensory profile." *American Journal of Occupational
Therapy* 61.2 (2007): 190-200.

Markram, K. "The Intense World Theory – A Unifying Theory of
the...." 2010.
<http://www.ncbi.nlm.nih.gov/pmc/articles/PMC3010743/>

Chapter 6

Farley, Megan A. et al. "Twenty-year outcome for idnividuals
with autism and average or near-average cognitive abilities."
Autism Research 2.2 (2009): 109-118.
Orsmond, Gael I, Marty Wyngaarden Krauss, and Marsha
Mailick Seltzer. "Peer relationships and social and
recreational activities among adolescents and adults with
autism." *Journal of Autism and Developmental Disorders* 34.3
(2004): 245-256.

Chapter 7

Baron-Cohen, Simon et al. "Prevalence of autism-spectrum
conditions: UK school-based population study." *The British
Journal of Psychiatry* 194.6 (2009): 500-509.
Kim, Young Shin et al. "Prevalence of autism spectrum disorders
in a total population sample." *American Journal of Psychiatry*
168.9 (2011): 904-912.
Taylor, Julie Lounds, and Marsha Mailick Seltzer. "Employment
and post-secondary educational activities for young adults
with autism spectrum disorders during the transition to
adulthood." *Journal of Autism and Developmental Disorders*
41.5 (2011): 566-574.
Taylor, Julie Lounds, and Marsha Mailick Seltzer. "Changes in
the autism behavioral phenotype during the transition to
adulthood." *Journal of Autism and Developmental Disorders*
40.12 (2010): 1431-1446.
Farley, Megan A. et al. "Twenty-year outcome for idnividuals
with autism and average or near-average cognitive abilities."
Autism Research 2.2 (2009): 109-118.
"ADA.gov homepage." 2003. 28 Nov. 2015
<http://www.ada.gov/>
"How These 4 Major Companies Are Tackling the Autism...."
2015. 28 Nov. 2015

<http://www.huffingtonpost.com/2015/05/07/autism-employment_n_7216310.html>

"Doctors are 'failing to spot Asperger's in girls' - The Guardian."
2013. 10 Jan. 2016
<http://www.theguardian.com/lifeandstyle/2009/apr/12/autism-aspergers-girls>

Chapter 8

Van Steensel, FJA. "Anxiety Disorders in Children and
Adolescents with Autistic...." 2011.
<http://www.ncbi.nlm.nih.gov/pmc/articles/PMC3162631/>

Ruta, L. "Obsessive-compulsive traits in children and
adolescents...." 2010.
<http://www.ncbi.nlm.nih.gov/pubmed/19557496>

Stewart, Mary E. et al. "Presentation of depression in autism and
Asperger syndrome - A review." *Autism* 10.1 (2006): 103-116.

Mayes, Susan Dickerson et al. "Suicide ideation and attempts in
children with autism." *Research in Autism Spectrum
Disorders* 7.1 (2013): 109-119.

Ghaziuddin, Mohammad, Neera Ghaziuddin, and John Greden.
"Depression in persons with autism: Implications for research
and clinical care." *Journal of Autism and Developmental
Disorders* 32.4 (2002): 299-306.

SERIES, OFC. "Autism Information for Child Abuse
Counselors." 2015. <http://www.autism-society.org/wp-content/uploads/2014/04/Child_Abuse_Counselors.pdf>

Chapter 9

"Facts and Statistics - Autism Society of America." 2014. 4 Jan.
2016 <http://www.autism-society.org/what-is/facts-and-statistics/>

"Doctors Largely Unprepared to Treat Adults on the Spectrum."
2015. 4 Jan. 2016

<https://www.disabilityscoop.com/2015/05/21/doctors-unprepared-spectrum/20323/>

"Special Report on Autism in Healthcare." 2015. 4 Jan. 2016 <http://www.certifiedautismspecialist.com/leading-autism-experts-release-special-report-on-autism-in-health-care-and-community-services/>

Nicolaidis, Christina et al. "Comparison of healthcare experiences in autistic and non-autistic adults: a cross-sectional online survey facilitated by an academic-community partnership." *Journal of General Internal Medicine* 28.6 (2013): 761-769.

"The missing generation | Spectrum - Autism Research News." 2015. 4 Jan. 2016 <https://spectrumnews.org/features/deep-dive/the-missing-generation/>

Venkat, Arvind et al. "Care of the patient with an autism spectrum disorder by the general physician." *Postgraduate Medical Journal* 88.1042 (2012): 472-481.

Made in the USA
Monee, IL
27 November 2020

49801713R00121